Communications
in Computer and Information

Alessandro Moschitti
Riccardo Scandariato (Eds.)

Eternal Systems

First International Workshop, EternalS 2011
Budapest, Hungary, May 3, 2011
Revised Selected Papers

 Springer

Volume Editors

Alessandro Moschitti
University of Trento
Department of Information Engineering and Computer Science
Via Sommarive 14, 38123 Povo, Italy
E-mail: moschitti@disi.unitn.it

Riccardo Scandariato
Katholieke Universiteit Leuven
Department of Computer Science
Celestijnenlaan 200A, 3001 Heverlee, Belgium
E-mail: riccardo.scandariato@cs.kuleuven.be

ISSN 1865-0929   e-ISSN 1865-0937
ISBN 978-3-642-28032-0   e-ISBN 978-3-642-28033-7
DOI 10.1007/978-3-642-28033-7
Springer Heidelberg Dordrecht London New York

Library of Congress Control Number: 2011945327

CR Subject Classification (1998): I.2, I.2.11, H.3-4, C.2, D.2, H.5.2

Typesetting: Camera-ready by author, data conversion by Scientific Publishing Services, Chennai, India

Printed on acid-free paper

Springer is part of Springer Science+Business Media (www.springer.com)

Preface

Methods to make systems capable of adapting to changes in user requirements and application domains are key ICT research areas. Adaptation and evolution depend on several dimensions, e.g., time, location, and security conditions, which express the diversity of the context in which systems operate. A design based on effective modeling of these dimensions constitutes a meaningful step toward the realization of *trustworthy eternal systems*.

The First International Workshop on Eternal Systems (EternalS 2011) was held on May 3, 2011, in Budapest, Hungary. The workshop was affiliated with the European Future Technologies Conference and Exhibition (fet^{11}) and sponsored by the European Coordination Action ETERNALS: Trustworthy Eternal Systems via Evolving Software, Data and Knowledge (www.eternals.eu).

EternalS 2011 aimed at creating the conditions for mutual awareness and cross-fertilization among broad ICT areas such as learning systems for knowledge management and representation, software systems, networked systems and secure systems, by focusing on their shared objectives such as adaptation, evolvability and flexibility for the development of long-living and versatile systems.

The workshop issued a call for high-quality contributions in the abovementioned areas and selected them by means of a peer review process, carried out by the major experts of the areas above. Out of the 15 submissions received, six full papers and four short papers were accepted for inclusion in this volume.

The Workshop Chairs would like to thank the authors who provided the content for this volume, and express their appreciation to the Program Committee members for their valuable work.

November 2011

Alessandro Moschitti
Riccardo Scandariato
Workshop Chairs

Organization

Workshop Organizers

Alessandro Moschitti   Università di Trento, Italy
Riccardo Scandariato   Katholieke Universiteit Leuven, Belgium

Program Committee

Roberto Basili	University of Rome Tor Vergara, Italy
Götz Botterweck	Lero, Ireland
Sofia Cassel	University of Uppsala, Sweden
Krishna Chandramouli	Queen Mary University of London, UK
James Clarke	Waterford Institute of Technology, Ireland
Anna Corazza	University of Naples Federico II, Italy
Sergio Di Martino	University of Naples Federico II, Italy
Michael Felderer	University of Innsbruck, Austria
Fausto Giunchiglia	University of Trento, Italy
Reiner Hähnle	Chalmers University, Sweden
Falk Howar	TU Dordtmund, Germany
Valerie Issarny	INRIA, France
Richard Johansson	University of Trento, Italy
Jan Jürjens	TU Dortmund, Germany
Paul Lewis	University of Southampton, UK
Ilaria Matteucci	CNR, Italy
Wolfgang Nejdl	L3S - University of Hannover, Germany
Claudia Niederee	L3S Research Centre, Germany
Julien Masanès	European Archive, France
Alessandro Moschitti	University of Trento, Italy
Animesh Pathak	INRIA, France
Tomas Piatrik	Queen Mary University of London, UK
Hongyang Qu	University of Oxford, UK
Rick Rabiser	JKU Linz, Austria
Riccardo Scandariato	Katholieke Universiteit Leuven, Belgium
Ina Schaefer	TU Braunschweig, Germany
Bernhard Steffen	TU Dortmund, Germany
Massimo Tivoli	University of L'Aquila, Italy
Daniel Varro	Budapest University of Technology, Hungary
Gerhard Weikum	Max-Planck-Institut fr Informatik, Germany
Qianni Zhang	Queen Mary University of London, UK

Table of Contents

Software and Secure Systems

Comparing Structure-Oriented and Behavior-Oriented Variability
Modeling for Workflows   1
    Anna-Lena Lamprecht, Tiziana Margaria, Ina Schaefer, and
    Bernhard Steffen

Towards Verification as a Service (Short Paper)   16
    Ina Schaefer and Thomas Sauer

Requirements-Driven Runtime Reconfiguration for Security
(Short Paper)   25
    Koen Yskout, Olivier-Nathanael Ben David,
    Riccardo Scandariato, and Benoit Baudry

Machine Learning for Software Systems

Large-Scale Learning with Structural Kernels for Class-Imbalanced
Datasets (Short Paper)   34
    Aliaksei Severyn and Alessandro Moschitti

Combining Machine Learning and Information Retrieval Techniques for
Software Clustering   42
    Anna Corazza, Sergio Di Martino, Valerio Maggio, and
    Giuseppe Scanniello

Reusing System States by Active Learning Algorithms   61
    Oliver Bauer, Johannes Neubauer, Bernhard Steffen, and Falk Howar

Ontology and Knowledge Representations

Inferring Affordances Using Learning Techniques (Short Paper)   79
    Amel Bennaceur, Richard Johansson, Alessandro Moschitti,
    Romina Spalazzese, Daniel Sykes, Rachid Saadi, and Valérie Issarny

Predicting User Tags Using Semantic Expansion   88
    Krishna Chandramouli, Tomas Piatrik, and Ebroul Izquierdo

LivingKnowledge: A Platform and Testbed for Fact and Opinion
Extraction from Multimodal Data.................................   100
    David Dupplaw, Michael Matthews, Richard Johansson, and
    Paul Lewis

Behaviour-Based Object Classifier for Surveillance Videos   116
    Virginia Fernandez Arguedas, Krishna Chandramouli, and
    Ebroul Izquierdo

Author Index   125

Comparing Structure-Oriented and Behavior-Oriented Variability Modeling for Workflows

Anna-Lena Lamprecht[1], Tiziana Margaria[2],
Ina Schaefer[3], and Bernhard Steffen[1]

[1] Chair for Programming Systems,
Technical University Dortmund, Germany
{anna-lena.lamprecht,bernhard.steffen}@cs.tu-dortmund.de
[2] Chair for Service and Software Engineering,
University Potsdam, Germany
tiziana.margaria@cs.uni-potsdam.de
[3] Institut für Software Systems Engineering,
Technische Universität Braunschweig, Germany
i.schaefer@tu-bs.de

Abstract. Workflows exist in many different variants in order to adapt
the behavior of systems to different circumstances and to arising user's
needs. Variability modeling is a way of keeping track at the model level
of the currently supported and used workflow variants. Variability modeling approaches for workflows address two directions: structure-oriented
approaches explicitly specify the workflow variants by means of linguistic constructs, while behavior-oriented approaches define the set of all
valid compositions of workflow components by means of ontological annotations and temporal logic constraints. In this paper, we describe how
both structure-oriented and behavior-oriented variability modeling can
be captured in an eXtreme Model-Driven Design paradigm (XMDD). We
illustrate this via a concrete case (a variant-rich bioinformatics workflow
realized with the jABC platform for XMDD), and we compare the two
approaches in order to identify their profiles and synergies.

1 Introduction

Workflows [1] express how to do things in practice, thus they are often subject
to ad-hoc changes, induced by evolving environments or needs, and resulting
in numerous related variants that address these slightly different needs. This
may easily lead to huge numbers of distinct workflows, which can be hardly
maintained individually. Hence, workflow modeling tools have to support the
variant-rich development of workflows. Accordingly, means for variability modeling and variability control help to systematically support the arising product
lines of processes in an economic and manageable fashion.

In order to reason about workflow variability and workflow configurations, explicit variability modeling concepts are necessary. Variability modeling provides

A. Moschitti and R. Scandariato (Eds.): EternalS 2011, CCIS 255, pp. 1–15, 2012.
© Springer-Verlag Berlin Heidelberg 2012

a precise overview of the currently supported and used workflow variants and allows to reason about the consistency and correctness of these variants. Two dimensions can be distinguished here in how to capture variability:

- *structure-oriented methods* specify explicitly variation points, i.e. those points of the model where functionality (workflow components) or parameter values have several alternatives. At each variation point, the attached variants represent different possibilities to realize the variation point. Concrete workflows arise then through selection of variants at given variation points. This is a very explicit way of handling variability.
- *behavior-oriented methods* instead constrain the combination of workflow components in a workflow through semantic annotations of the components, as well as rules and constraints that govern the proper combination of these components in terms of their semantic annotations. This is a more liberal, declarative, and indirect way of handling variability.

Clearly, the structure-oriented hierarchical variability modeling approach is a variability modeling concept originating from software product line engineering [2] and similar to the feature models [3, 4] in use in that community.

The behavior-oriented variability modeling approach has a semantic and decision-management touch that is in good alignment with the XMDD paradigm of [5, 6]. There, one tends to manage decisions by using properties (expressed as constraints) that must hold on process models, and tools that either check (for instance by model checking) or enforce (by automatic generation and synthesis) those properties on the artifacts (hierarchical process models) and their transformations (e.g. from models to code). The jABC [7] is a framework for service-oriented modeling and design of processes and workflows that supports semantic annotations, model checking, and automatic synthesis of workflows according to the *loose programming* paradigm of [8].

While the structure-oriented approach is mainstream, the behavioral approach is conceptually new in this context (see Sect. 5). In this paper, we explore for the first time both approaches, with the goal of understanding their profiles (strengths and weaknesses) and identifying possible synergies. The XMDD paradigm should in principle be able to accommodate both approaches, and the jABC should be able to offer both after some extensions with functionality to capture the structural description of variation points and variants explicitly.

The remainder of the paper is structured as follows: In Section 2, we describe the case example used throughout this paper. We present a structural and behavioral approach to modeling workflow variability in Sections 3 and 4, respectively. Subsequently, Section 5 briefly reviews related work, and Section 6 elaborates on the profile of the two considered approaches to variability and provides some perspectives.

2   Case Example

We use the bioinformatics workflow of [9], which is variant-rich and has been already implemented in the jABC, as a case example for our investigations.

select sequence file   read sequence file   show alignment

ClustalW

Fig. 1. Simple bioinformatics workflow, computing a multiple sequence alignment

In its basic form, the user selects a file containing a molecular sequence, that is, a DNA or protein sequence. The content of the file is then read and sent to the ClustalW web service of the DDBJ [10]. (ClustalW [11] is a popular algorithm for computing multiple alignments from molecular sequences.) Finally, the computed alignment is displayed to the user in a text dialog window. As there are naturally different ways to obtain input data (e.g., from local files, from remote databases, via manual input), different ways to compute alignments (different algorithms as well as different service providers), and different ways to handle the obtained results (e.g., direct display, saving as a file, storage to a database, using it as input for subsequent computations), several variations of this workflow can be directly derived (cf. [9]). In this paper, we use the variability of this example workflow to illustrate the difference between the structural and the behavioral variability modeling concepts.

The concrete modeling we use is shown in Figure 1 for the basic workflow. The basis for the model in jABC are libraries of semantically annotated workflow components, called *SIBs* (*Service Independent Building Blocks*). SIBs provide units of functionality. The first SIB (**read sequence file**, at the left) displays a file chooser dialog window, where the user selects the file of the molecular sequence to be processed. SIBs can be freely combined into flowchart-like workflow structures called *Service Logic Graphs*, or *SLGs*. The SLG of this simple workflow contains four SIBs: it starts at the left SIB (the underlined name denotes that this is the Start SIB of the process), the selected file is then read (SIB **read sequence file**), sent to the **ClustalW** web service of the DDBJ platform in Japan, and the result is displayed to the user in a text dialog window (SIB **show alignment**).

3   Structure-Oriented Variability Modeling

Structure-oriented variability modeling uses linguistic constructs that extend the modeling language to describe all possible variants of a workflow. We apply here the concept of *hierarchical variability modeling* [12] to express the variability of (nested) workflows. Hierarchical variability modeling was developed in the context of software product line engineering [2]. There, it expresses via syntactic constructs the variability of the artifacts that are reused to build the different products of a product line. Hierarchical variability modeling separates the variability description of the artifacts in different hierarchical layers in order to allow for a structured and modular representation of the artifacts and their (nested) variations.

In a hierarchical variability model now applied to workflows, on each hierarchical layer we need to capture and make explicit in the model what is the commonality and what is the variability of the considered workflow instances at that layer. Accordingly, a *common core workflow* represents the commonality of all defined workflow instances. The common core workflow, as every ordinary jABC workflow, is an SLG. It contains workflow components, i.e., SIBs, and connections between these SIBs. Additionally, the core workflow may contain *variable workflow components*, i.e., SIBs that represent *variation points* in the workflow. Variation points describe steps where the workflow execution may vary. The variation point SIBs in the common core workflow are therefore 'placeholders' for one of the alternatives. A workflow containing variation points is called a *variable* workflow, otherwise the workflow is *concrete*.

Each variable workflow component has a set of associated *variants* which represent how the variability introduced by the variation points can be realized. A variant can be a concrete workflow component or a subworkflow that may contain variable workflow components itself, such that it creates a new hierarchical layer in the variability model. Given a variable workflow description, a concrete workflow instance can be derived from it by selecting the variants for each variable workflow component. The set of all workflow instances that can be derived by variant selection is the *variability space* defined by the structure-oriented hierarchical variability model.

Of course, not all selections of variants at all variation points give rise to a sensible workflow instance, due to dependencies. Often certain variants can only be combined with specific other variants, while some variants require the selection of other variants at particular variation points. In hierarchical variability modeling, these *diversity constraints* are specified by *requires- and excludes-constraints* between variants associated to different variation points. A requires-constraint between two variants states that one variant requires the selection of the other variant. An excludes-constraint between two variants states that the selection of one variant prevents the selection of another variant. Additionally, the selection of some variants may be optional.

In order to ensure that a hierarchical variability model only defines executable workflows, it has to satisfy certain well-formedness constraints. The common core workflow containing variable workflow components has to ensure that the allowed compositions of the workflow components have compatible inputs and outputs. A simple means to ensure the input/output constraints is to require that all variants have the same inputs and outputs, a constraint which is easily checkable. A less restrictive alternative is to consider the diversity constraints when checking the input and output constraints. This is more flexible, but it is also more difficult to check, because in the worst case all possible workflow instances satisfying the diversity constraints must be checked.

In the following, we illustrate how the hierarchical variability model described above can elegantly express variants of the simple alignment workflow of Figure 1. In order to stay within the graphical modeling style proposed by XMDD, we extend the graphical notation of the jABC with constructs that represent

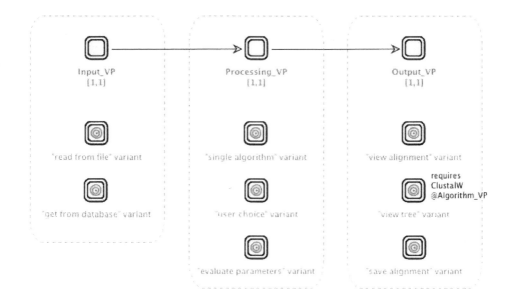

Fig. 2. Variable workflow

variation points by variable workflow components and the associated variants. As mentioned before, the common core workflows are ordinary jABC workflows possibly containing variable workflow components that specify variation points. Thus, we need to show how to express common core workflows, how to represent variable workflow components, and how to show the association between a variable workflow component and its variants.

Fig. 3. Read from file variant

In our example, Figure 2 depicts the top hierarchical level of the variable bioinformatics workflow. The common core workflow is the connected portion of the SLG. It consists of three major steps: input, processing, and output. Each of these three steps offers variants, which is expressed by the three variation points that we identify on this level, named Input_VP, Processing_VP, and Output_VP. The variants associated to each variation point are graphically included inside a dashed rounded box. In this example, the cardinality annotation [1,1] for each variation point specifies that exactly one of the respective variants has to be selected. Variants are workflows themselves, and they can again contain variation points. For the input variation point, for instance, we see that it is either possible to read the input sequences from a local file (with the concrete workflow of Figure 3, as chosen in the simple workflow of Fig. 1), or to retrieve a set of sequences from a remote database.

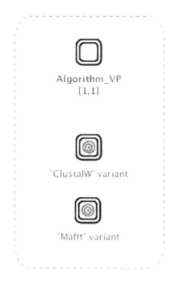

Fig. 4. Single algorithm variant

For the processing variation point, there are variants that use a single algorithm, that let the user choose an algorithm at runtime, or that evaluate different parameter configurations of an alignment algorithm. The variant for using a single algorithm is depicted in Figure 4: It does not contain a common core workflow, but only another variation point with associated variants for the ClustalW and the Mafft alignment algorithms. In contrast, the parameter evaluation variant shown in Figure 5 contains a common core workflow, expressing that the alignment is carried out with all possible values for a particular parameter in order to determine which value leads to the best alignment. Within this variant, the single algorithm variation point defined above is reused in order to make the evaluate parameters variant parametric in the actually used alignment algorithm.

Finally, for the output variation point, the different variants available offer the choice between viewing the alignment, viewing the implied phylogenetic tree, and saving the alignment result to a file. As we see in Fig. 2, the tree visualization variant is only applicable when the ClustalW variant is selected for the algorithm variation point, because only the ClustalW result contains the information necessary for the tree visualization steps - the other alignment algorithms do not provide this information. This dependency is captured by the

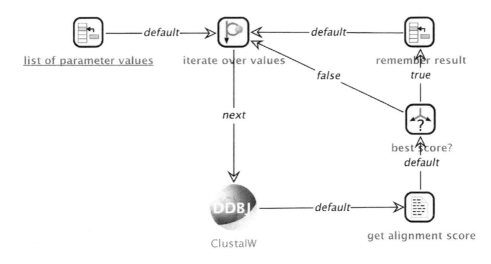

list of parameter values   iterate over values   remember result

Fig. 5. Evaluate parameters variant

requires constraint attached to the **view tree** variant. As we described previously, these constraints restrict the freedom in choosing individual variants to those alternatives that make sense in the global context.

As we see, the structure-oriented hierarchical variability modeling approach facilitates the explicit representation of variability within the workflow definition. Using this approach, the variability contained in a workflow definition can be intuitively specified. The common structures of all workflow instances can be easily understood by considering only the common core workflows at each hierarchical layer. By focusing on the different variants, it is easy to see which concrete workflow components are required to realize the specified set of workflow instances.

The modular variability representation (simply "next to each other" on the canvas) increases the scalability of the modeling approach towards large and complex workflows by allowing the separate modeling of variable nested sub-workflows associated to different variation points. Reused (variable) workflows are indeed modeled only once. The hierarchical model structure further allows compositional reasoning: one can ensure workflow properties by analyzing each hierarchical level in isolation, due to some restrictions on their global interplay in terms of diversity constraints. Hierarchical variability modeling also supports the evolution of workflow descriptions, since variants that become newly available can be added to variation points without changing other parts of the variability model.

In this sense, structure-oriented variability modeling is in good alignment with the principles of XMDD, including the "One-Thing-Approach" [6], which enforces a global view on the modeled system that goes from the overview to the details, down the workflow hierarchy, and strictly reuses available sub-workflows and SIBs (the well known "write things once" commandment).

4   Behavior-Oriented Variability Modeling

The XMDD paradigm has been designed to support a semantics-based approach for service-oriented modeling and design of processes and workflows. Aiming at a service-oriented implementation that uses libraries of artifacts (services, or component libraries, or APIs of existing legacy code), the basis for the behavioral models are libraries of semantically annotated workflow components, (in the case of jABC, the *SIBs*), that provide particular units of functionality. These units can be orchestrated into flowchart-like workflow structures (the SLGs in the jABC case). In XMDD, the semantics helps to define a space of legal behavioral variants, by enhancing the model layer with a second kind of description, in terms of properties. At any time, the current design can be checked against those properties, which express the envelope of the desired or legal behaviors. The conceptual idea of the semantics-oriented variability modeling approach builds on this philosophy: start with all possible combinations of the available workflow components, and restrict them by adding constraints, thereby defining the variability space.

This definition of the admissible workflows in the behavior-oriented approach is based on the *loose programming* paradigm (see [8] for a detailed introduction). Loose programming enables developers to design their application-specific workflows in an intuitive style. Key to this approach is the concept of loose specification, a graphical formalism that allows expressing workflows just by sketching them as flow graphs without caring initially about input/output compatibility (because there is a mechanism in the background that inserts type converters and adapters if necessary), or precise knowledge about the available workflow components or the availability of resources (meaning here the availability of data provided by previous components). Developers only have to specify a rough process flow graphically in terms of a combination of ontologically defined workflow components. Concretely, SIBs as well as data types are semantically classified, and their use and instantiation must respect the consistency at the semantic level, too. This way, one is guaranteed to obtain SLGs (manually or with synthesis support) that are "correct" with respect to the current ontology of components and data and to the current set of constraints.

These loose specifications are then concretized to fully executable workflows automatically by means of a combination of 1) data-flow analysis, ensuring the availability of the required resources, 2) temporal logic-based process synthesis, resolving type conflicts and taking care of correct component instantiation, and 3) model checking, to ensure global intents and invariants expressed in temporal logic.

In order to support the *loose programming paradigm* [8], the jABC contains tool support for formal methodology (provided by the GEAR model checking plugin [13] and the PROPHETS plugin for logic-based process synthesis [14]) to ensure that the SLGs do not violate the constraints that characterize the intended variability space, that is, the set of all valid workflows. Loose

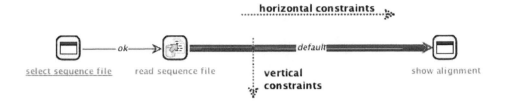

Fig. 6. Alignment worfklow with a loosely specified branch

programming seems thus best equipped to allow also variability to be expressed as a constraint, and treated with the existing tools as a new dimension of constraints and knowledge.

As an example for the semantics-oriented variability modeling approach, consider the loosely specified workflow in Figure 6, where the SIBs `read sequence file` and `show alignment` are connected by a (red-colored, bold) loose branch. In order to handle this loose specification by the formal methodology described above, the loose specification is translated into a set of temporal logic formulas[1]. More specifically, these constraints are expressed in terms of the Semantic Linear Time Logic (SLTL) [15], a variant of Linear Time Logic (LTL) that combines the usual operators for relative time (next, eventually, until, ...) with ontological classifications of types and services: atomic propositions and actions are not simply "labels" but range over the ontology associated with the components.

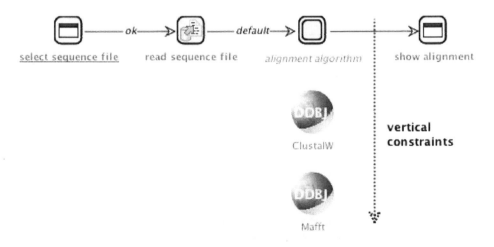

Fig. 7. Alignment worfklow with variants according to vertical constraints (ontological terms)

---

[1] Additional constraints for loose specifications that further restrict the admissible compositions can simply be given by additional formulas. The set of constraints is in this sense compositional.

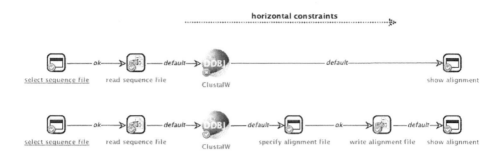

Fig. 8. Alignment worfklow with variants according to horizontal constraints (temporal logic formulas)

Accordingly, in this setup, two dimensions of constraints can be distinguished:

- *Vertical constraints* are basically abstract type or service descriptions in terms of ontologies, that is, constraints that specify which components can be instantiated at a certain variation point[2]. The semantic annotations of the SIBs in the jABC are provided in terms of simple ontologies. For instance, the `ClustalW` SIB from our example is classified as *alignment algorithm* in the ontology. The SLTL constraint

$$F < \texttt{alignment algorithm} > true$$

(intuitively, this translates to "finally, there is an *alignment algorithm* step") uses this ontological term to express that the workflow has to comprise a SIB from this ontological class. This is de facto a description of the variation point for single algorithms that now is described using terms of the ontology. The result is shown in Figure 7.
- Orthogonally, the *horizontal constraints* typically constrain the temporal and causal relationship between components and variation points and are given in terms of temporal logics. Adapting the examples given above, a horizontal constraint could, for instance, express that every computed ClustalW alignment has to be stored to the local file system (for later use). Formally, this can be expressed as

$$G(< \texttt{ClustalW} > true \Rightarrow X(F(< \texttt{write file} > true)))$$

(presence of `ClustalW` at any point implies that subsequently the workflow must contain also a file writing step). Thus, concretizations for the loose branch that only consist of `ClustalW` would not be sufficient to meet this constraint, whereas those that incorporate also the file-saving steps would be valid (cf. Figure 8).

---

[2] A variation point in structure-oriented variability modeling has essentially the same meaning.

Both kinds of constraints can be combined in order to express more complex specifications. This allows for a very flexible fine-tuning of valid variations:

- The intent of a workflow can be comfortably specified in terms of temporal logic formulas without unnecessarily constraining the concrete realization. For instance, a possible combination of constraints similar to those shown above is needed when requiring to save the results of any kind of *alignment algorithm* to a file - that is, the different possible variants do not have to be stated explicitly and the specification does not have to be changed if, e.g., new SIBs are added to the ontology.
- Frame conditions and type-constraints can be either modeled in terms of so-called local constraints (for specifying allowed components in an intended workflow), or in terms of temporal formulas (for global properties, like intents).

Due to the power of temporal logics, this constraints-based descriptive style allows specifications ranging from very coarse requirements, like "no business object should be used that has not been introduced", to very tight constraints that determine the workflow up to bisimulation [16]. Thus, it is possible to describe the intended range of workflows in a very flexible fashion, while at the same time it can be formally proved whether a certain concrete workflow satisfies the variability constraints via model checking [17, 18].

The approach is, however, not limited to validate workflow instances relative to the corresponding variability model. Rather, it is also possible to validate general properties of the variability model itself. In fact, once properly set up, it is possible to guarantee that each workflow refining the constraint-based variability model is immediately executable, or that it obeys a certain important policy.

More elaborate is the use of temporal synthesis [19, 20] to automatically treat constraint violations either by proposing possible repairs or by directly repairing the workflow based on defaults. This approach has been successfully applied already in the '90s for the variation management of so-called value-added services [21]. In the meantime it has been generalized and improved to cover less rigidly designed application domains like bioinformatics [22–24]

5 Related Work

There is very little related work on behavioral variability modeling, even though there was already an industrially successful solution in the mid-'90s for the variation management of so-called value-added services. There, libraries of constraints specified the according variability space, and led to drastically reduced times to market. Most advanced was the approach presented in [21], where the idea of modal transition systems was used to intuitively constrain the variability space, and to guarantee that newly created variants can be deployed without any further testing.

In contrast, the amount of related work on structural variability modeling is vast. Variability in requirements analysis is predominantly captured by features models [4], whose features are end-user visible product functionalities. Using a special syntax for denoting mandatory and optional features and additional selection constraints, the set of valid feature combinations is defined. This set relates to the set of admissible products, but features are only labels relating to functionalities [3]. Alternatively, at the level of requirements analysis variability is represented by decision-oriented variability modeling [25].

The existing syntax-oriented approaches to represent variability on the artifacts level can be classified into three main directions [26]. First, annotative approaches consider one model representing all products of a product line. Variant annotations, e.g., using UML stereotypes [27, 28], presence conditions [29], or separate variability representations, such as orthogonal variability models [2], define which parts of the model have to be removed to derive the model of a concrete product.

Second, compositional approaches associate product fragments with product features which are composed for particular feature configurations. A prominent example for the compositional approach is AHEAD [30], where a product is built by stepwise refinement of a base module with a sequence of feature modules. In [26, 31, 32], models are constructed by aspect-oriented modeling techniques. [33] applies model superposition to compose model fragments.

Third, transformational approaches, such as [34], represent variability by rules determining how modeling elements of a base model have to be replaced for a particular product model. Delta modeling [35] is another instance of transformational variability modeling where a set of systems is described by a designed core system and a set of system deltas modifying the core system.

Hierarchical variability modeling, as presented in this paper, generalizes the ideas of the Koala component model [12] for the implementation of variant-rich component-based systems to the requirements and design phase. In Koala, the variability of a component is described by the variability of its sub-components which can be selected by so called *switches* via explicit *diversity interfaces*, information about selected variants is communicated between sub- and supercomponents. Diversity interfaces and switches in Koala can be understood as concrete language constructs targeted at the implementation level to express variation points and associated variants. Plastic partial components [36] are an architectural modeling approach where component variability is defined by extending partially defined components with variation points and associated variants. However, variants cannot contain variable components, so that this modeling approach is not truly hierarchical.

6   Conclusion and Perspectives

We have presented a structure-oriented and behavior-oriented variability modeling approach, and illustrated that they both can be elegantly captured in an eXtreme Model-Driven Design paradigm (XMDD) by considering the variant-rich bioinformatics workflow realized in [9] with the jABC platform. It is apparent that the two approaches have complementary strength, which we will briefly summarize according to expressive power, analyzability, and support of evolution.

In the structure-oriented approach, the variability space is modeled explicitly in an architectural or "shoe-box"-style by explicitly listing the valid alternatives for the variation points, which is very intuitive and immediately understandable. Essentially, this turns the corresponding analysis into a combinatorial problem, where the various instances are checked explicitly. The number of these checks is typically reduced by a locality principle: vital dependencies are only allowed to appear at a given level within a certain (sub)model. Evolution is typically simply realized by adding more alternatives for certain variation points, or by extending the variability model, e.g., by adding further variation points.

In contrast, in the behavior-oriented approach the variability space is described via temporal constraints and loose ontological component specifications, which defines the set of possible workflows extensionally. As a consequence, properties of variability models can be verified via logical implication, and the validity of a certain concrete workflow instance via model checking. Evolution of a variability model is simply a matter of varying the defining constraints.

From a broader perspective, these different profiles lead to another significant difference: whereas structural variability models can only be sensibly related when they are structurally similar, behavioral variability models can flexibly be related according to logical implication, which leads to powerful variation libraries, and to the fact that established properties are automatically inherited along the implication chains. This has already been exploited more than 10 years ago for the modeling of value-added telecommunication services for a fast development of new product lines, which required strong structural changes, but whose behavioral specifications remained quite similar [21].

Currently we are investigating how the advantages of the two variability approaches can be combined in order to arrive at an easy-to-understand, yet flexible variability modeling framework. For example, we have found that behavior-oriented variability modeling can in fact simplify feature modeling [37]. In this line, we also consider other structure- oriented variability-modeling approaches, such as delta modeling [35], and methods for supporting the generation of concrete workflow instances, for instance using temporal logic synthesis in the fashion described in [8].

References

1. van der Aalst, W.M.P., van Hee, K.: Workflow Management: Models, Methods and Systems. MIT Press (2002)
2. Pohl, K., Böckle, G., van der Linden, F.: Software Product Line Engineering - Foundations, Principles, and Techniques. Springer, Heidelberg (2005)
3. Czarnecki, K., Eisenecker, U.W.: Generative Programming: Methods, Tools, and Applications. Addison-Wesley (2000)
4. Kang, K., Lee, J., Donohoe, P.: Feature-Oriented Project Line Engineering. IEEE Software 19(4) (2002)

5. Margaria, T., Steffen, B.: Agile IT: Thinking in User-Centric Models. In: Margaria, T., Steffen, B. (eds.) Leveraging Applications of Formal Methods, Verification and Validation. CCIS, vol. 17, pp. 490–502. Springer, Heidelberg (2009)
6. Margaria, T., Steffen, B.: Business Process Modelling in the jABC: The One-Thing-Approach. In: Handbook of Research on Business Process Modeling. IGI Global (2009)
7. Steffen, B., Margaria, T., Nagel, R., Jörges, S., Kubczak, C.: Model-Driven Development with the jABC. In: Bin, E., Ziv, A., Ur, S. (eds.) HVC 2006. LNCS, vol. 4383, pp. 92–108. Springer, Heidelberg (2007)
8. Lamprecht, A.L., Naujokat, S., Margaria, T., Steffen, B.: Synthesis-Based Loose Programming. In: Proceedings of the 7th International Conference on the Quality of Information and Communications Technology, QUATIC (September 2010)
9. Lamprecht, A.-L., Margaria, T., Steffen, B.: Seven Variations of an Alignment Workflow - An Illustration of Agile Process Design and Management in Bio-jETI. In: Măndoiu, I., Wang, S.-L., Zelikovsky, A. (eds.) ISBRA 2008. LNCS (LNBI), vol. 4983, pp. 445–456. Springer, Heidelberg (2008)
10. Kwon, Y., Shigemoto, Y., Kuwana, Y., Sugawara, H.: Web API for biology with a workflow navigation system. Nucl. Acids Res. 37(suppl_2), W11–W16 (2009)
11. Larkin, M., Blackshields, G., Brown, N., Chenna, R., McGettigan, P., McWilliam, H., Valentin, F., Wallace, I., Wilm, A., Lopez, R., Thompson, J., Gibson, T., Higgins, D.: Clustal W and Clustal X version 2.0. Bioinformatics 23(21), 2947–2948 (2007)
12. van Ommering, R.C.: Software reuse in product populations. IEEE Trans. Software Eng. 31(7), 537–550 (2005)
13. Bakera, M., Margaria, T., Renner, C., Steffen, B.: Tool-supported enhancement of diagnosis in model-driven verification. Innovations in Systems and Software Engineering 5, 211–228 (2009), doi:10.1007/s11334-009-0091-6
14. Naujokat, S.: Automatische Generierung von Prozessen im jABC. Diplomarbeit, TU Dortmund (September 2009)
15. Steffen, B., Margaria, T., Freitag, B.: Module Configuration by Minimal Model Construction. Technical report, Fakultät für Mathematik und Informatik, Universität Passau (1993)
16. Milner, R.: Communication and concurrency. Prentice-Hall, Inc., Upper Saddle River (1989)
17. Clarke, E.M., Grumberg, O., Peled, D.A.: Model Checking. The MIT Press (1999)
18. Müller-Olm, M., Schmidt, D., Steffen, B.: Model-Checking - A Tutorial Introduction. Static Analysis, 848 (1999)
19. Manna, Z., Wolper, P.: Synthesis of Communicating Processes from Temporal Logic Specifications. ACM Trans. Program. Lang. Syst. 6(1), 68–93 (1984)
20. Steffen, B., Margaria, T., von der Beeck, M.: Automatic synthesis of linear process models from temporal constraints: An incremental approach. In: ACM/SIGPLAN Int. Workshop on Automated Analysis of Software, AAS 1997 (1997)
21. Braun, V., Margaria, T., Steffen, B., Yoo, H., Rychly, T.: Safe service customization. In: Intelligent Network Workshop, IN 1997, vol. 2, p. 4. IEEE (1997)
22. Lamprecht, A.L., Margaria, T., Steffen, B.: Bio-jETI: a framework for semantics-based service composition. BMC Bioinformatics 10(suppl.10), S8 (2009)
23. Lamprecht, A.L., Naujokat, S., Margaria, T., Steffen, B.: Semantics-based composition of EMBOSS services. Journal of Biomedical Semantics 2(suppl. 1), S5 (2011)

24. Lamprecht, A.L., Naujokat, S., Steffen, B., Margaria, T.: Constraint-Guided Workflow Composition Based on the EDAM Ontology. In: Burger, A., Marshall, M.S., Romano, P., Paschke, A., Splendiani, A. (eds.) Proceedings of the Workshop on Semantic Web Applications and Tools for Life Sciences, CEUR Workshop Proceedings, Berlin, Germany, December 10, vol. 698 (2010)
25. Schmid, K., Rabiser, R., Grünbacher, P.: A comparison of decision modeling approaches in product lines. In: VaMoS, pp. 119–126 (2011)
26. Völter, M., Groher, I.: Product Line Implementation using Aspect-Oriented and Model-Driven Software Development. In: SPLC, pp. 233–242 (2007)
27. Ziadi, T., Hélouët, L., Jézéquel, J.M.: Towards a UML Profile for Software Product Lines. In: Workshop on Product Familiy Engineering (PFE), pp. 129–139 (2003)
28. Gomaa, H.: Designing Software Product Lines with UML. Addison Wesley (2004)
29. Busch, C.: Overview of Generative Software Development. In: Banâtre, J.-P., Fradet, P., Giavitto, J.-L., Michel, O. (eds.) UPP 2004. LNCS, vol. 3566, pp. 326–341. Springer, Heidelberg (2005)
30. Batory, D., Sarvela, J., Rauschmayer, A.: Scaling Step-Wise Refinement. IEEE Trans. Software Eng. 30(6), 355–371 (2004)
31. Heidenreich, F., Wende, C.: Bridging the Gap Between Features and Models. In: Aspect-Oriented Product Line Engineering, AOPLE 2007 (2007)
32. Noda, N., Kishi, T.: Aspect-Oriented Modeling for Variability Management. In: SPLC (2008)
33. Apel, S., Janda, F., Trujillo, S., Kästner, C.: Model Superimposition in Software Product Lines. In: Paige, R.F. (ed.) ICMT 2009. LNCS, vol. 5563, pp. 4–19. Springer, Heidelberg (2009)
34. Haugen, Ø., Møller-Pedersen, B., Oldevik, J., Olsen, G., Svendsen, A.: Adding Standardized Variability to Domain Specific Languages. In: SPLC (2008)
35. Clarke, D., Helvenstcijn, M., Schaefer, I.: Abstract delta modeling. In: GPCE. Springer, Heidelberg (2010)
36. Pérez, J., Díaz, J., Soria, C.C., Garbajosa, J.: Plastic Partial Components: A solution to support variability in architectural components. In: WICSA/ECSA, pp. 221–230 (2009)
37. Schaefer, I., Lamprecht, A.L., Margaria, T.: Constraint-oriented Variability Modelin. In: Rash, J., Rouff, C. (eds.) 34th Annual IEEE Software Engineering Workshop (SEW-34). IEEE CS Press (to appear, 2011)

Towards Verification as a Service

Ina Schaefer[1] and Thomas Sauer[2]

[1] Technische Universität Braunschweig,
Braunschweig, Germany
i.schaefer@tu-bs.de
[2] rjm business solutions GmbH,
Lampertheim, Germany
t.sauer@rjm.de

Abstract. Modern software systems are highly configurable and evolve over time. Simultaneously, they have high demands on their correctness and trustworthiness. Formal verification technique are a means to ensure critical system requirements, but still require a lot of computation power and manual intervention. In this paper, we argue that formal verification processes can be cast as workflows known from business process modeling. Single steps in the verification process constitute verification tasks which can be flexibly combined to verification workflows. The verification tasks can be carried out using designated services which are provided by highly scalable computing platforms, such as cloud computing environments. Verification workflows share the characteristics of business processes such that well-established results and tool support from workflow modeling, management and analysis are directly applicable. System evolution causing re-verification is supported by workflow adaptation techniques such that previously established verification results can be reused.

1 Introduction

Modern computer systems are getting more and more complex. They exist in several different variants at one point in time in order to adapt to different customer needs. Furthermore, modern software systems are extremely long-lived and evolve in order to adjust to changing user or environment requirements. Additionally, software systems are designed to dynamically adapt their behavior and internal structure according to changes in the environment, e.g., to recover from failures or to optimize their functionality with respect to the available resources. At the same time, these systems have are high requirements on their correctness and trustworthiness, since they control essential functionality in medical, automotive or industrial-control applications. Hence, despite system diversity, it is crucial to ensure that in every possible system configuration at any point in time, critical safety and security requirements are met.

Formal methods are a means to rigorously ensure these requirements [12]. However, formal verification still requires a lot of manual effort and computation power. One particular problem is that automatic verification techniques,

A. Moschitti and R. Scandariato (Eds.): EternalS 2011, CCIS 255, pp. 16–24, 2012.

such as model checking [5], do not scale for large and complex systems. To counter this problem, verification complexity reduction techniques, such as compositional reasoning [7] or model transformations [4], have been proposed. These techniques increase the applicability of formal verification, but require manual intervention. Thus, formal verification of modern large-scale software systems that allows to keep up with the market pressure has not yet been achieved.

In this paper, we argue that formal verification processes involving the application of verification complexity reduction techniques can be cast as workflows. Workflows describe the execution of process activities in a structured way and are a well-known concept from business process modeling [13]. The steps in the verification process, i.e., the application of different verification complexity reductions and the actual calls to verification tools, can be captured as verification tasks. These verification tasks may then be flexibly composed into a verification workflow, which describes the best possible way to achieve a reduction of verification complexity. The verification workflow is executed via services that carry out the individual verification tasks. When these services are provided by a service-oriented computing environment, such as a highly scalable cloud computing platform, computation resources are in many cases no longer an issue. The formulation of verification processes as verification workflows has the following benefits:

- Verification workflows share the same characteristics as business process, such that existing techniques and tools from workflow modeling, management and analysis [13] can be directly applied. This eases the specification and verification of complex verification processes and facilitates automated workflow execution.
- Verification processes can be executed as flexible services in service-oriented computing environments, such as cloud computing platforms [14]. Cloud computing platforms provide sheer unlimited computing resources on demand at reasonable cost. This alleviates restrictions for completing computationally expensive analyses. The large-scale distribution of the verification tasks is taken care of by the service-oriented computing environment which allows flexibly replacing services if more efficient ones become available.
- If the system and the properties to be verified evolve over time, workflow adaptation and re-planning techniques [10] can be applied to reuse previously established verification results. The flexibility provided by service-oriented computing environments further simplifies re-planning of verification processes.

This paper is structured as follows: In Section 2, we review related work on workflows as well as on service-oriented computing and model-based verification. In Section 3, we present the novel verification as a service approach. Section 4 illustrates the proposed approach at the model-based verification of adaptive embedded systems. Finally, Section 5 summarizes this paper with an outlook to future work.

2   Related Work

The term *workflow* commonly refers to the automation of a business process [6]. A business process describes a structured approach for reaching a commercial goal, e.g., for producing goods. A workflow is formed by a set of self-contained tasks and their interdependencies, such that information can be passed among the participants as required.

Design, analysis, and reuse of workflows have been subject to intense research in the last years [13]. For workflow design, a rich variety of process description languages is available which allows specifying individual tasks as well as their compositions. Besides control flow aspects, such as parallelism and synchronization, workflow design typically covers a common representation of task results and resource allocation aspects. Workflow analysis techniques allow ensuring consistency and correctness of the specified workflows, e.g., the absence of dead-locks or live-locks [13]. Most approaches translate workflow descriptions to a formal representation, such as Petri nets, and apply formal reasoning techniques in order to ensure properties of the workflows. Workflow evolution due to changing requirements has been discussed in the context of adaptive or agile workflows [10] in order to provide methodologies for syntactically and semantically correct workflow adaptation.

Workflows can be executed in service-oriented computing environments which abstract from the concrete task scheduling and distribution. The *Service-Oriented Architecture (SOA)* approach perceives all computational resources as services that can be dynamically discovered and composed [15]. The individual tasks of a workflow can be conceived as such services. The SOA approach eases the integration of heterogeneous systems and applications built using different technologies or software infrastructures. In particular, this allows flexibly allocating the most suitable services to execute tasks and alleviates the complexity in case of workflow evolution. A common approach for implementing a SOA uses *web services* which make the desired functionality programmatically accessible over standard Internet protocols.

Cloud computing is a recent trend to implement service-oriented computing environments [14]. Cloud computing refers to a shared, extremely powerful processing infrastructure provided over an abstract interface, such that the actual location and management of processing nodes is of no concern. Ideally, many organizations share the same infrastructure such that it can be used economically.

A concept similar to verification workflows that are presented in this paper are *scientific workflows* describing structured activities and computations that arise in scientific problem-solving [9], for instance in bioinformatics [8]. The SAL [2] and IF [3] verification frameworks, similar to the model-based verification framework presented in [11], apply various verification complexity reduction techniques, such as slicing and abstractions, in order to enable the formal verification of large-scale system. However, neither of these approaches presents a workflow for capturing how the different reduction techniques should be carried out, but leave this as a manual activity.

3   Verification as a Service

Verification as a Service (VaaS) is a novel approach based on the notion of verification workflows, which can be executed on a service-oriented computing environment. The VaaS approach is illustrated in Figure 1. Starting from a system and properties to be verified, a verification workflow is devised, arranging verification tasks in a suitable ordering. This verification workflow can be executed on a service-oriented computing environment providing analysis as well as verification complexity reduction services. In the following, we explain the different steps in detail.

3.1   Verification Workflows

For specifying verification processes as workflows, we first identify the verification tasks that are part of the process. The concrete tasks depend on the considered application scenario. In general, verification tasks are characterized by their inputs and outputs and a functional description. If verification tasks refer to verification complexity reductions, property-preservation theorems are required which ensure that only the size of the verification problem is changed, but the validity of the property to be established is not affected. The tasks involved in a verification process are usually the following:

1. *Decomposition/Composition:* Using compositional reasoning, the verification of a global property over a complete system can be decomposed into a set of smaller verification problems requiring verification of local properties over parts of the system. The validity of the local properties implies the validity of the global property. If the decomposition yields additional constraints, such as assumptions in case of assume-guarantee reasoning [7], also for discharging these constraints verification problems are generated. In case the

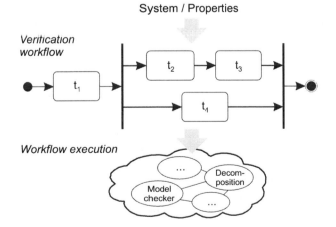

Fig. 1. Verification as a Service

validity of the global property depends on the local properties, the local verification results are combined to the global verification result in a composition verification task.

2. *Projection:* Usually, not all parts of a system contribute to the validity of a property such that the complete system can be reduced only to the relevant parts, e.g., a subset of components in a component-based system.

3. *Abstraction:* If a system is too large to be verified directly, abstraction provides a means to reduce this complexity while retaining the essential system behavior for the validity of the property. If computations are performed on a large and infinite data domain, system data and computations can be abstracted to a finite abstract domain that is sufficiently precise to establish the desired property.

4. *Translation:* If the verification complexity reductions are carried out on an intermediate system representation, the verification problems have to be translated to the input language of the used verification tools. Similarly, the results returned from the verification tools have to be translated back to the intermediate representation language in order to allow the system developer to trace back failures, e.g., error traces produced by model checkers.

5. *Analysis:* The verification problems are solved by verification tools, such as model checkers, static analyzers or theorem provers, which represented by analysis tasks. In order to facilitate the automatic execution of the verification workflows, these analyses have to be automatized.

The verification tasks can be flexibly composed to form a verification workflow by using a process description language, e.g., the one used in [10]. Within a verification workflow, the individual verification tasks may be arranged in sequence such that one task is executed after the other. Further, an AND-split construct allows for parallel execution of verification tasks, e.g., when a decomposition results in several independent verification problems. A corresponding AND-join then yields that the workflow execution is synchronized at this point. In addition, verification workflows may contain XOR-split constructs to express case distinctions in the workflow execution. Finally, loops enable the repetitive execution of verification tasks.

The concrete ordering in which the verification tasks can be composed depends on the application scenario. The composition of the verification tasks can be optimized to maximize the parallel execution of sub-workflows or the amount of the verification complexity reduction that can be achieved. Alternatively, the computational resources required can be minimized. In general, the workflow composition has to ensure that the outputs provided and the inputs required by the verification tasks are compatible. Furthermore, the result of the completed verification workflow has to be correct, which means that the obtained verification result is correct. These properties can be verified by applying existing workflow analysis and verification technique to the verification workflow itself, which constitutes another verification workflow which can be handled by the same means.

3.2   Workflow Execution

Once the verification workflow is fully specified, it can be executed by an service-oriented execution environment which takes care of distribution and scheduling of verification tasks. Each of the verification tasks are executed by designated service in the execution environment. The services are specified by service descriptions. A service description, amongst others, contains a name, a specification of the service functionality and a specification of the required inputs and provided outputs. Service descriptions typically comprise a service level agreement (SLA) stating the provided service quality. For instance, in an SLA it could be captured that the service provides a certificate that the computed results are correct.

The execution platform determines appropriate services capable for carrying out each of the verification tasks by comparing service descriptions with the respective task characterizations. For example, analysis tasks are mapped to services which encapsulate calls to verification tools. Depending on the actually used execution platform, automatic service discovery by means of semantic matchmaking is enabled. This allows to flexibly add and remove services based on their availabilty, which greatly simplifies deployment of both platform and services.

It is important that the result of executing a verification workflow is correct. This includes that the verification tasks are executed in the exact ordering as specified by the verification workflow and that the services are appropriately selected for the verification tasks and compute correct results. To ensure this, service-oriented computing environments often adhere to SLAs which ensure the quality of the provided services. Additionally, the certificates provided by the services can be checked after verification workflow execution to validate the computed results. If the service-oriented computing environment is implemented on a cloud computing platform, trust in the verification results can be guaranteed by using a private cloud where full control over the services and the execution ordering is ensured.

3.3   Evolution

When the system and the properties to be verified evolve due to changing requirements, the verification workflow must be adapted accordingly. For example, additional tasks or further case distinctions may become necessary, while others get obsolete. Techniques for workflow adaptation [10] support re-planning of the verification workflow such that the resulting workflow is again syntactically and semantically correct.

In many cases the workflow adaptation can be optimized such that previously obtained verification results can be reused. Instead of having to repeat all verification steps, only the changed portions of the verification workflows are executed. This leads to significant performance gains if, e.g., only single components have been modified.

4   Application Scenario

In the following, we illustrate the verification as a service approach at the model-based verification of adaptive embedded systems [11]. Adaptation (or graceful degradation) is used in modern cars in order to improve safety and reliability in case of sensor failure. Adaptive embedded systems are designed by a composition of reconfigurable components. Each of these components has a number of pre-determined functional configurations that are selected depending on the component's environment. The adaptation behavior of the complete system emerges from the composition of the reconfigurable components. An adaptation in one component may trigger adaptations in other components which in turn may cause further adaptations. An important property of the adaptation behavior is that adaptation stabilizes after a finite number of adaptation steps if the quality of the system inputs stays stable.

In [11], a model-based verification framework for ensuring critical properties of the adaptation behavior is proposed where design-level models of adaptive embedded systems are translated to a formal semantics-based intermediate representation. Critical properties of the adaptation behavior can be formulated in temporal logics and verified by existing model checkers [1]. In general, the considered systems are too complex to be directly amenable to automatic verification. Hence, a set of verification reduction techniques are applied. Compositional reasoning strategies, including assume-guarantee reasoning, allow splitting large and complex verification problems into a set of smaller verification problems for components of the system. Slicing techniques enable reductions to only those components that contribute to the validity of a property. Data domain abstraction facilitate reducing infinite data domains to finite abstract domains. Finally, property-preservation theorems ensure for all above mentioned reduction strategies that the properties to be verified are preserved under the performed transformations.

The verification process for adaptive embedded systems suggested in [11] can be stated as a verification workflow. In order to obtain the best possible verification complexity reduction, it is advisable to perform decompositions as early as possible followed by slicing and abstraction steps. Figure 2 depicts a workflow for an exemplary verification process. The first step is a decomposition of the system S_0 into two separate system parts S_1 and S_2, for which two independent properties have to be established. For the first property, the verification complexity is reduced via a slicing task, before the verification problem is translated to the input of a verification tool and analyzed. For the second property, an abstraction step is performed followed by a translation and an analysis task.

While in [11], the verification process is a manual effort guided by a wizard-like GUI, the verification as a service approach enables the automatic execution of the verification process by a service-oriented computing environment. When realized by cloud computing, the significant computational resources required especially for the analysis tasks can be provided in the cloud at affordable cost.

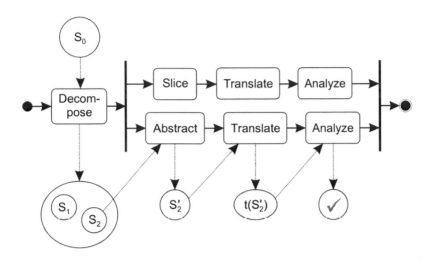

Fig. 2. Example Verification Workflow

5   Conclusion and Future Work

In this paper, we argued that verification processes should be cast as workflows. This allows using existing techniques for workflow design and analysis to specify and verify verification processes leading to the best possible reduction of verification complexity. Based on service-oriented computing environments, verification workflows can be automatically executed with the necessary computation resources. Workflow adaptation techniques provide a means to re-plan verification processes to accommodate system and property evolution.

A prerequisite for formulating verification processes as workflows is that the verification goal can be split into a number of tasks that can be solved distributedly by a number of verification services. Furthermore, verification has to be as automatic as possible in order to minimize user interactions. In particular, this makes the verification as a service approach useful for the model-based model-based verification of adaptive embedded systems. However, the proposed approach is not restricted to such systems, but is rather applicable to any domain sharing similar characteristics.

There are many directions for future work. First, in order to ensure the correctness of verification workflows, existing workflow analysis techniques have to be adapted to reason over verification tasks. For increasing trust in the obtained verification results, strategies for certifying verification services as well as infrastructure and platform providers need to be investigated. In order to support the automatic construction of verification workflows from a set of given verification tasks, semantics-oriented modeling approaches following the loose programing paradigm [8] can be applied. According workflow evolution, further research is planned on the systematic reuse of verification results.

References

1. Adler, R., Schaefer, I., Schuele, T., Vecchié, E.: From Model-Based Design to Formal Verification of Adaptive Embedded Systems. In: Butler, M., Hinchey, M.G., Larrondo-Petrie, M.M. (eds.) ICFEM 2007. LNCS, vol. 4789, pp. 76–95. Springer, Heidelberg (2007)
2. Bensalem, S., Ganesh, V., Lakhnech, Y., Munoz, C., Owre, S., Ruess, H., Rushby, J., Rusu, V., Saidi, H., Shankar, N., Singerman, E., Tiwari, A.: An Overview of SAL. In: Fifth NASA Langley Formal Methods Workshop (LFM), pp. 187–196 (2000)
3. Bozga, M., Graf, S., Ober, I., Ober, I., Sifakis, J.: The IF Toolset. In: Bernardo, M., Corradini, F. (eds.) SFM-RT 2004. LNCS, vol. 3185, pp. 237–267. Springer, Heidelberg (2004)
4. Clarke, E., Grumberg, O., Long, D.: Model Checking and Abstraction. ACM Trans. Prog. Lang. Syst. 16(5), 1512–1542 (1994)
5. Clarke, E., Grumberg, O., Peled, D.: Model Checking. MIT Press (1999)
6. Hollingsworth, D.: The workflow reference model. Technical report, WfMC, Document TC-1003 (1995)
7. Kupferman, O., Vardi, M.: Modular Model Checking. In: Compositionality: The Significant Difference, Int'l Symposium, pp. 381–401 (1997)
8. Lamprecht, A.-L., Margaria, T., Steffen, B.: Bio-jETI: a framework for semantics-based service composition. BMC Bioinformatics (2009)
9. Ludäscher, B., Altintas, I., Berkley, C., Higgins, D., Jaeger, E., Jones, M., Lee, E.A., Tao, J., Zhao, Y.: Scientific workflow management and the kepler system. Concurrency and Computation: Practice & Experience 18, 1039–1065 (2006)
10. Sauer, T., Minor, M., Bergmann, R.: Inverse workflows for supporting agile business process management. In: Proceedings of the 6th Conference on Professional Knowledge Management. LNI, vol. 182, pp. 204–213 (2011)
11. Schaefer, I.: Integrating Formal Verification into the Model-based Development for Adaptive Embedded Systems. PhD thesis, University of Kaiserslautern (2008)
12. Schaefer, I., Hähnle, R.: Formal methods in software product line engineering. IEEE Computer 44(2), 82–85 (2011)
13. van der Aalst, W.M.P., van Hee, K.: Workflow Management: Models, Methods and Systems. MIT Press (2002)
14. Wei, Y., Blake, M.B.: Service-oriented computing and cloud computing: Challenges and opportunities. IEEE Internet Computing 14(6), 72–75 (2010)
15. Zhang, L.-J., Zhang, J., Cai, H.: Services Computing. Springer, Heidelberg (2007)

Requirements-Driven Runtime Reconfiguration for Security

Koen Yskout[1], Olivier-Nathanael Ben David[2],
Riccardo Scandariato[1], and Benoit Baudry[2]

[1] IBBT-DistriNet, Katholieke Universiteit Leuven, Belgium
koen.yskout@cs.kuleuven.be
[2] INRIA, France
olivier-nathanael.ben_david@inria.fr

Abstract. The boundary between development time and run time of eternal software intensive applications is fading. In particular, these systems are characterized by the necessity to evolve requirements continuously, even after the deployment. In this paper we focus on the evolution of security requirements and introduce an integrated process to drive runtime reconfiguration from requirements changes. This process relies on two key proposals: systematic strategies to evolve architecture models according to security requirements evolution and the combination of reflective middleware and models@runtime for runtime reconfiguration.

Keywords: security, evolution, software architecture, requirements, runtime.

1 Introduction

The requirements of a system are subject to continuous change. For instance, changes occur when the stakeholders of the system request new functionality, when new technologies appear or when the system has to adapt to new categories of users. Also, the reuse of the system in a different environment or context can lead to changes in the requirements. These changes are even more prominent in open, eternally running systems that have to continuously adapt to new environments.

A change in the requirements ultimately leads to changes in the running system. Sometimes, small changes in the implementation of the system suffice to cover the updated requirements. Often, however, a change in the requirements has a deep impact on the structure of the system. Additionally, the boundary between development time and runtime is fading [3] in the context of eternal software intensive systems. In front of all these constraints, we are interested in two major challenges: (i) systematically reflect requirements changes in the system's architecture and (ii) automatically reconfigure the system according to architectural changes, without stopping it.

In this paper we focus on security requirements that will represent a major challenge for open eternal systems that integrate complex interaction between

A. Moschitti and R. Scandariato (Eds.): EternalS 2011, CCIS 255, pp. 25–33, 2012.

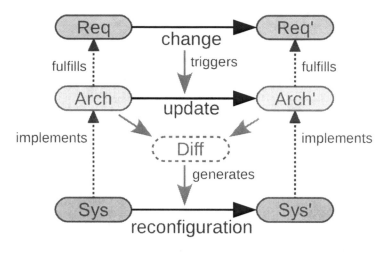

Fig. 1. Overview

users, mobile devices and sensitive data and services. We sketch an integrated solution to deal with dynamic system reconfiguration driven by requirements changes. The proposed solution relies on two key elements: (1) the introduction of change patterns to reflect security requirements changes in component-based models and (2) models@runtime to dynamically reconfigure the running system according to changes in the architecture. Figure 1 graphically displays this global process.

The top part of Figure 1 illustrates a change in the requirements that triggers an update in the architecture model. Evolving an architecture in order to satisfy new requirements is an extremely difficult problem. In this work we want to rely on the notion of change patterns as principled strategies to update the architecture according to recurring change scenarios in security requirements.

The bottom part of Figure 1 illustrates a system reconfiguration that is driven by the architecture update. This reconfiguration is based on a (`Diff`) operation that computes the difference between two architectures. As a result of this operation, it is possible to know how a system that conforms to the initial architecture must be changed in order to satisfy the target architecture. On this basis it is possible to generate a sequence of middleware commands to performs the reconfiguration.

In the rest of this paper we present more details that support the feasibility of such an integrated process. Section 2 introduces the notion of change patterns and Section 3 presents a possible mechanism for reconfiguration based models@runtime. Section 4 summarizes some related work and Section 5 discusses challenges for future work that will aim at realizing this integrated security reconfiguration process.

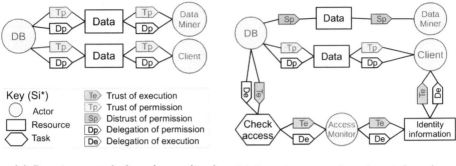

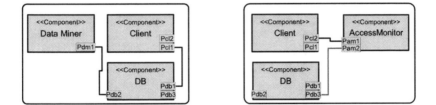

(a) Requirements before change (Req)   (b) Requirements after change (Req')

(c) Architecture before change (Arch)   (d) Architecture after change (Arch')

Fig. 2. Sample requirements change and corresponding adaptation

2   Change Patterns

As an illustration for this paper, consider a simple system that consists of a database (DB) and a client application (e.g., a GUI) for this database. Moreover, the data from the database is used by a data miner. The client is initially trusted, as it is used only by a single, trusted user. Therefore, the client has permission to access all data in the database. Similarly, the data miner is trusted with its permission to access the data. This situation is represented in the initial requirements model Req in Figure 2(a) using the Si* notation [4], which is particularly suited to express trust relationships.

Assume that, over time, additional users begin to work with the client application. In such scenario, the client can no longer be trusted by the database. Therefore, the system needs to change in order to deal with the new situation, and the trust relationship from the requirements model should be modified to a distrust relationship. For the sake of illustration, assume that the data miner coincidentally abuses the data it receives, and becomes distrusted as well.

In order to reconcile the architecture with the requirements, at least two options exist. The most drastic solution is to completely deny access to the data, which amounts to removing (or blocking) the communication path with the database. In the example, this solution is applied to the data miner.

For the client application it would be unacceptable, as the client's sole purpose is to communicate with the database. Therefore, a second solution is chosen for the client, namely limiting its possibilities for misbehavior by monitoring access to the database and enforcing an access control policy. The client only gets permission to access a specific subset of the data, based on the identity of the user and other constraints. The resulting requirements model `Req'`, after introducing both solutions, is shown in Figure 2(b).

Figure 2(c) represents the initial architecture `Arch` of the example. This is the architecture that fulfills the initial requirements `Req`, and contains three components: 'Client', 'Data Miner' and 'DB'. The 'Client' component connects to the 'DB' component to allow the end user to work with the database. The 'Data Miner' component connects to the database as well, in order to extract data for data mining purposes.

The updated architecture `Arch'` is shown in Figure 2(d), and corresponds to the updated requirements `Req'` from before. The 'Client' and 'DB' components are kept in place. However, an 'AccessMonitor' component is added between them, to check whether a client is authorized to access the requested data. If access is granted, and only then, a binding between 'AccessMonitor' and 'DB' is added and the 'AccessMonitor' provides (forwards) the information to the client. This binding is represented in blue between the ports Pam2 and Pdb3. Since the communication path between the 'Data Miner' and 'DB' component is removed, as discussed before, the 'Data Miner' component is also removed from `Arch'`.

Numerous types of changes can occur at the requirements level, one of which is the decreasing trust in the preceding example. This type of change is not only relevant for the given example, but will occur in the context other systems as well. Moreover, it is likely that the solutions given above are also applicable in these other contexts.

The combination of a change at the requirements level and one or more architectural updates can be bundled in the form of a change pattern. It is related to a specific kind of change at the requirements level, which is described in a generic manner, i.e., using templates. In the example, this change is the change of a trust to a distrust relationship between the system (the DB) and an external actor (the Client and Data Miner). The pattern also offers guidance on how the described change impacts the architecture, again in a generic way based on templates. The generic description of the change between `Arch` and `Arch'` in the example is 'disconnect and remove the component that corresponds to the distrusted actor' (used for the data mining), or 'introduce an access control monitor' (used for the client application). Like well-known design patterns, change patterns thus inform a software architect about common, proven solutions for specific problems. Additionally, the patterns should provide information regarding their applicability, benefits and possible pitfalls when applying them.

Of course, the update of the architecture needs to be propagated to the running system. This is done using reconfiguration, which is discussed in the following section.

3   Reconfiguration

In this section we introduce an automated mechanism to dynamically reconfigure a system that implements an initial architecture, according to a target architecture model. Starting from both architectural models Arch and Arch', we propose to leverage models@runtime and the reconfiguration process proposed by Morin [6]. The process leverages reflective middleware capabilities and allows to generate and apply a reconfiguration script to adapt a system that conforms to Arch into a system that conforms to Arch'.

The first step in the reconfiguration process consists of comparing the reflective model of the running system with Arch. If they are different, it means that the initial architectural model does not correspond to the running system, and thus that the system cannot be updated according to the update from Arch to Arch'. If the models are the same, the second step consists of comparing Arch and Arch'. This comparison allows to understand which reconfiguration operations (i.e., change a binding, or add / remove a component) must be performed on the system so that it conforms to Arch'. When performing the update, it needs to be ensured that:

- All the elements of the source model that have a matching counter part in the target model are kept;
- All elements of the source model that have no matching counter part in the target model will be removed;
- All the elements of the target model that have no matching counter part in the reflection model will be added.

On the basis of this comparison, the third step consists in generating a sequence of reconfiguration commands. The exact command language available for dynamic reconfiguration depends on the possibilities provided by the reflective dynamic middleware platform (e.g., OSGi, OpenCOM or Fractal). Morin has implemented this process in Kermeta [8] to generate a reconfiguration script for the OSGi component platform. During the model comparison, the comparator uses an abstract factory to instantiate atomic reconfiguration commands These commands are not directly executed, and so the running system is not adapted during the model comparison. The commands are temporarily stored and sorted, before the whole sequence of commands is actually executed. That allow to use planning algorithms to sort them. A simple heuristic is used to sort the reconfiguration commands :

1. Components (that should be stopped) are stopped;
2. Bindings are removed;
3. Components are removed;
4. Attributes (of already present components) are updated;
5. Components are added (and their attributes are set);
6. Bindings are added;
7. Components are (re-)started.

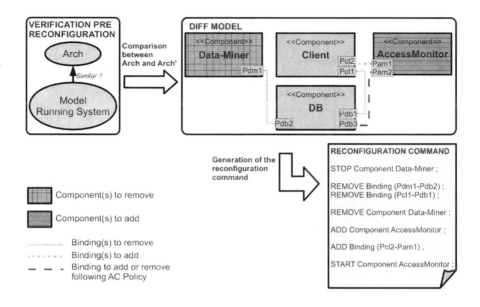

Fig. 3. Generation of reconfiguration command

In addition, each type of command is associated with a real value defining its priority. By default, the priority is a natural integer following the above enumeration. However, it is possible to modify this priority by adding a real value in $[0..1[$ to the default value for fine-tuning the order of the commands within a given category without modifying the overall ordering. This topological sort ensures that the life-cycle of the components is correctly handled. The order inside a given type of commands is arbitrary, except for start and stop commands. These commands are ordered according to the client/server dependencies of components.

After the model comparison, and all the commands have be instantiated, the whole sequence of commands is executed. A command is only executed if the previous one correctly terminates. In the case a command encounters a problem, the reconfiguration process stops and a report is properly logged. A roll-back mechanism allows to undo the command that crashes, as well as all the previous ones to avoid cascades of errors.

4 Related Work

The term 'change pattern' is already established in the context of business process modeling [5,11]. There, however, a change pattern is used to capture modifications to a single process model, whereas we use it to co-evolve different models.

The presented approach is related to techniques aimed at, on the one hand, updating the architectural model of a system in reaction to a change request, and on the other hand, adapting the running system to a new architecture. References to related work in both areas are given in the following two subsections.

4.1   Architectural Evolution

To guide the gradual transition from one architecture to another, Garlan et al. [2] propose the concept of 'evolution styles'. An evolution style is a pattern that can be used by the architect to plan incremental evolution paths (orthogonal to the evolution of functional requirements) from an initial architecture to some target architecture.

Graph transformations have also been used to model architectural evolution. In [10], Tamzalit and Mens describe how architectural restructuring can be described using graph transformations. In particular, the approach is tailored for defining generic restructurings that introduce an architectural style, called *evolution patterns*.

Ráth et al. [9] describe an approach for incremental model synchronization, based on change-driven model transformations. The technique is not specific to architectural models, but nevertheless applicable to them. When the source model (e.g., a requirements model) is modified, a description of this change (called the 'change history model') is created. This change history model is transformed to a different change history model, specific for the target metamodel, and then applied to the target model (e.g., the architectural model).

4.2   Run-Time Adaptability

Bencomo et al. in [1] present Genie, a tool that offers DSLs for the design of models of component configurations and transition diagrams. These models describe the architecture of reconfigurable applications and the conditions of the environment and context that trigger the reconfiguration of the architecture.

Morin et al. in [7] describe how to unify design evolution and runtime adaptation of dynamically adaptive systems in order to build consistent adaptation decisions. On the conceptual side, their approach combines Complex Event Processing, Model Driven Engineering and Context-aware systems. Thus they have presented a monitoring framework able to deal with both design evolution events and run-time platform events in a homogeneous manner.

5   Conclusion and Outlook

In summary, change patterns provide principled strategies for evolving an architecture in response to a security change in the corresponding requirements. By leveraging reconfiguration, we illustrated how change can be systematically propagated beyond the architectural design, that is, from the requirements level to the runtime environment. As a key outcome, the end-to-end traceability links provide an infrastructure to validate that the runtime system complies with the security requirements over time.

In general, this is a very challenging problem due to the intellectual gap that exist between the problem and the solution domains. In this respect, the use of the change patterns reduces the scope of the problem, as compliance needs to be demonstrated for a limited, fixed set of configurations. Namely, the system's architecture after the change (`Arch'`) needs to be constrained so that it fulfills the changed requirements (`Req'`). In many cases, no precise semantics are defined for this fulfillment relationship, and hence the validation mostly needs to be done manually. However, for the cases where such precise definition is available, it is possible to formally prove that some architectural update, when applied to an architecture `Arch` that fulfills the original requirements `Req`, will result in an architecture `Arch'` that fulfills the updated requirements `Req'`, perhaps under some additional assumptions.

In the horizontal dimension, the system's architecture after the change also needs to be constrained, in ways that are independent from the specific requirements. In particular, architectural properties need to be preserved by the change. In these cases, the verification relies on invariant checking in `Arch'`. Invariants can take the form of OCL constraints, which in turn can be checked thanks to the Kermeta metamodeling language. It should also be possible to define different checking levels, depending of what invariants are intended to be checked. Examples are invariants related to the architecture, the specific platform, or the application.

The end result of combining the validation in both the vertical and the horizontal dimensions is a more rigorous change management infrastructure for security that goes beyond assurance and approach correctness. Our ongoing and future work will progress along this very trajectory.

Acknowledgements. This research is partially funded by the NESSoS FP7 project, the Interuniversity Attraction Poles Programme Belgian State, Belgian Science Policy, and by the Research Fund K.U.Leuven.

References

1. Bencomo, N., Grace, P., Flores, C., Hughes, D., Blair, G.: Genie: Supporting the model driven development of reflective, component-based adaptive systems. In: Proceedings of the 30th International Conference on Software Engineering, pp. 811–814. ACM (2008)
2. Garlan, D., Barnes, J., Schmerl, B., Celiku, O.: Evolution styles: Foundations and tool support for software architecture evolution. In: Proceedings of the Joint Working IEEE/IFIP Conference on Software Architecture 2009 & European Conference on Software Architecture 2009, pp. 131–140 (2009)
3. Ghezzi, C.: The fading boundary between development time and run time. Invited talk for the 6th International Symposium on Software Engineering for Adaptive and Self-Managing Systems (2011)

4. Giorgini, P., Massacci, F., Zannone, N.: Security and Trust Requirements Engineering. In: Aldini, A., Gorrieri, R., Martinelli, F. (eds.) FOSAD 2005. LNCS, vol. 3655, pp. 237–272. Springer, Heidelberg (2005)
5. Kim, D., Kim, M., Kim, H.: Dynamic business process management based on process change patterns. In: International Conference on Convergence Information Technology, pp. 1154–1161. IEEE (2007)
6. Morin, B.: Leveraging Models from Design-time to Runtime to Support Dynamic Variability. Ph.D. thesis, cole doctorale Matisse (2010)
7. Morin, B., Ledoux, T., Ben Hassine, M., Chauvel, F., Barais, O., Jézéquel, J.M.: Unifying runtime adaptation and design evolution. In: IEEE 9th International Conference on Computer and Information Technology (CIT 2009), Xiamen, China (October 2009)
8. Muller, P.-A., Fleurey, F., Jézéquel, J.-M.: Weaving Executability into Object-Oriented Meta-Languages. In: Briand, L.C., Williams, C. (eds.) MoDELS 2005. LNCS, vol. 3713, pp. 264–278. Springer, Heidelberg (2005)
9. Ráth, I., Varró, G., Varró, D.: Change-Driven Model Transformations. In: Schürr, A., Selic, B. (eds.) MODELS 2009. LNCS, vol. 5795, pp. 342–356. Springer, Heidelberg (2009)
10. Tamzalit, D., Mens, T.: Guiding Architectural Restructuring through Architectural Styles. In: 2010 17th IEEE International Conference and Workshops on Engineering of Computer-Based Systems, pp. 69–78. IEEE (2010)
11. Weber, B., Rinderle, S., Reichert, M.: Change Patterns and Change Support Features in Process-Aware Information Systems. In: Krogstie, J., Opdahl, A.L., Sindre, G. (eds.) CAiSE 2007 and WES 2007. LNCS, vol. 4495, pp. 574–588. Springer, Heidelberg (2007)

Large-Scale Learning with Structural Kernels for Class-Imbalanced Datasets

Aliaksei Severyn and Alessandro Moschitti

Department of Computer Science and Engineering,
University of Trento,
Via Sommarive 5, 38123 POVO (TN), Italy
{severyn,moschitti}@disi.unitn.it

Abstract. Much of the success in machine learning can be attributed to the ability of learning methods to adequately represent, extract, and exploit inherent structure present in the data under interest. Kernel methods represent a rich family of techniques that harvest on this principle. Domain-specific kernels are able to exploit rich structural information present in the input data to deliver state of the art results in many application areas, e.g. natural language processing (NLP), bio-informatics, computer vision and many others. The use of kernels to capture relationships in the input data has made Support Vector Machine (SVM) algorithm the state of the art tool in many application areas. Nevertheless, kernel learning remains a computationally expensive process. The contribution of this paper is to make learning with structural kernels, e.g. tree kernels, more applicable to real-world large-scale tasks. More specifically, we propose two important enhancements of the approximate cutting plane algorithm to train Support Vector Machines with structural kernels: (i) a new sampling strategy to handle class-imbalanced problem; and (ii) a parallel implementation, which makes the training scale almost linearly with the number of CPUs. We also show that theoretical convergence bounds are preserved for the improved algorithm. The experimental evaluations demonstrate the soundness of our approach and the possibility to carry out large-scale learning with structural kernels.

Keywords: Machine Learning, Kernel Methods, Structural Kernels, Support Vector Machine, Natural Language Processing.

1 Introduction

Different domain-specific kernels have been successfully applied to various Natural Language Processing (NLP) tasks, e.g. [10,13,9,1]. However, previous work scales poorly to the real-world datasets, where the number of examples is typically in the order of millions. Indeed, kernel methods require to carry out learning in dual spaces, where training complexity is typically quadratic in the number of instances.

To reduce such training time [16] proposed an approximate version of the cutting plane algorithm (CPA) [14] for training SVMs with general kernels. [12]

A. Moschitti and R. Scandariato (Eds.): EternalS 2011, CCIS 255, pp. 34–41, 2012.

showed that the same algorithm can be successfully applied to train SVMs with structural kernels on very large data obtaining speedup up factors up to 10. These studies employ 1-slack optimization problem reformulation [5], which is much faster than conventional cutting plane methods on large-scale datasets and produces sparser solutions.

Unfortunately, the 1-slack reformulation prevents to accomplish cost-sensitive classification using a standard approach in SVMs, i.e. outweighing the positive or negative errors. This is a critical drawback for applications in NLP where data is often imbalanced, which requires optimization of Precision/Recall measures.

In this paper, we provide two important improvements of the approximate CPA that enable the use of structural kernels, e.g. tree kernels, for large-scale learning: (i) an effective and sound method for tuning up Precision and Recall on imbalanced datasets and (ii) parallelization of the training algorithm improving its scalability even further. Regarding the application side, we show that our method allows for experimenting with tree kernels on very large real-world datasets such as Yahoo! Answers.

The experimental results confirm the validity of our approach as (i) it greatly outperforms previous approximate CPA when tuning of P/R is needed and (ii) it still matches the F_1-score of exact SVMs. Regarding the running time evaluation: our approach is as fast as CPA with sampling and, when parallelized, the speedup scales almost linearly with the number of available CPUs.

2   Cutting Plane Algorithm with Sampling

Let us consider an equivalent reformulation of SVM QP training problem, known as a 1-slack reformulation, which produces a much more efficient version of the CPA [5]:

$$\begin{aligned}
&\underset{\boldsymbol{w},\xi\geq 0}{\text{minimize}} \quad \frac{1}{2}\|\boldsymbol{w}\|^2 + C\xi \\
&\text{subject to} \quad \frac{1}{n}\sum_{i=1}^{n} c_i y_i \boldsymbol{w} \cdot \boldsymbol{x}_i \geq \frac{1}{n}\sum_{i=1}^{n} c_i - \xi, \\
&\quad \forall \boldsymbol{c} \in \{0,1\}^n
\end{aligned} \tag{1}$$

where each vector $\boldsymbol{c} \in \{0,1\}^n$ forms all possible linear combinations of the classical constraints $y_i(\boldsymbol{w}\cdot\boldsymbol{x}_i) \geq 1 - \xi_i$.

The key benefit of this reformulation is that there is only a single slack variable ξ that is now shared across all the constraints. Even though the number of constraints swelled up to 2^n, the cutting plane method (Alg. 1) requires only a sufficient subset of constraints S to solve the problem (1). It works by iteratively resolving QP (line 4) over the current set S and adding a new constraint $\boldsymbol{c}^{(t)}$ violated the most by the current solution $\boldsymbol{w}$ (lines 5-7) until no constraints are violated by more than ϵ (line 10).

When using kernels, examples are mapped to the feature space via a mapping $\phi(\cdot)$ and finding the most violated constraint (lines 5-7) involves computing an

---

Algorithm 1. Cutting Plane Algorithm (primal)

1: Input: $(\boldsymbol{x}_1, y_1), \ldots, (\boldsymbol{x}_n, y_n)$, C, ϵAlg.
2: $S \leftarrow \emptyset; t = 0$
3: **repeat**
4:    $(\boldsymbol{w}, \xi) \leftarrow$ optimize (1) over the constraints in S
      /* find a cutting plane */
5:    **for** $i = 1$ to n **do**
6:       $c_i^{(t)} \leftarrow \begin{cases} 1 \ y_i(\boldsymbol{w} \cdot \boldsymbol{x}_i) \leq 1 \\ 0 \ otherwise \end{cases}$
7:    **end for**
      /* add a constraint to the set of constraints */
8:    $S \leftarrow S \cup \{\boldsymbol{c}^{(t)}\}$
9:    $t = t + 1$
10: **until** $\frac{1}{n} \sum_{i=1}^{n} c_i^{(t)}(1 - y_i \boldsymbol{w} \cdot \boldsymbol{x}_i) \leq \xi + \epsilon$
11: **return** w, ξ

---

inner product between the weight vector and each training example: $\boldsymbol{w} \cdot \phi(\boldsymbol{x}_i)$. In the dual space, where $\boldsymbol{w}$ expands over the dual variables $\boldsymbol{\alpha}$, this inner-product renders as:

$$\boldsymbol{w} \cdot \phi(\boldsymbol{x}_i) = \sum_{k=1}^{n} \left(\sum_{t=1}^{|S|} \frac{1}{n} \alpha_t c_k^{(t)} y_k \right) K(\boldsymbol{x}_i, \boldsymbol{x}_k), \tag{2}$$

where $K(\boldsymbol{x}_i, \boldsymbol{x}_k) = \phi(\boldsymbol{x}_i) \cdot \phi(\boldsymbol{x}_i)$ is a kernel[1]. Computing (2) for each training example requires $O(n^2)$ kernel evaluations which makes the CPA training of non-linear SVMs no better than conventional decomposition methods.

To address this limitation [16] proposed to approximate the expensive computation of the most violated constraint over the full set of training examples n by using a smaller sample r. In this case the expensive double sum of kernel evaluations at each iteration reduces from $\sum_{i,j=1}^{n} K(\boldsymbol{x}_i, \boldsymbol{x}_j)$ to a more tractable: $\sum_{i,j=1}^{r} K(\boldsymbol{x}_i, \boldsymbol{x}_j)$, such that the most violated constraint is effectively computed over a smaller set of examples uniformly sampled from the original training set. Even though at each step we compute only an approximation of the exact cutting plane, the sampling approach has been shown to provide accurate solutions and converge in a finite number of steps irrespective of the training set size.

3   Improving CPA with Sampling

In this section we present two improvements to the CPA with sampling: (i) we propose an alternative sampling strategy that is effective for tuning up Precision and Recall and (ii) we parallelize the training algorithm.

---

[1] due to the space constraints, for a more careful treatment of the dual version of CPA with kernels we refer the reader to [8] or [12].

3.1 Sampling Strategy for Imbalanced Data

To address the problem of the imbalanced data one idea can be to use different penalty factors [15] C^+ and C^- for examples from positive and negative classes. This modification is easy to incorporate into the standard soft-margin SVM formulation where we have individual slack variables ξ_i for each constraint.

However, when using the 1-slack formulation (1), we have a single slack variable shared across all the constraints, while in the dual each α_i no longer corresponds to the individual example but to a linear combination of examples. This makes the task of controlling class imbalance through different margin parameters C^+ and C^- non-trivial. On the other hand the idea of sampling to approximate (2) at each iteration suggests a straight-forward solution. Instead of uniformly sampling r examples to compute the most violated constraint at each step, we can use cost-proportionate rejection sampling technique. This

---

Algorithm 2. Rejection sampling

1: Pick example $(\boldsymbol{x_i}, y_i, q_i)$ at random
2: Flip a coin with bias q_i/q'
3: **if** *heads* **then**
4:    keep the example
5: **else**
6:    discard it
7: **end if**

---

technique is presented in Alg. 2, where q_i is the importance weight of the i-th example and q' is an upper bound on any importance value in the dataset. This process is repeated until we sample the required number of examples. This modification enables the control over the proportion of examples from different classes that will form a sample used to compute the most violated constraint. Unlike the conventional approaches for addressing the class-imbalance problem, that either under-sample the majority class or over-sample the minority class from the training data, the rejection sampling coupled with cutting plane algorithm does not discard any examples from the training set. At each iteration we form a sample according to the pre-assigned importance weights for each example, such that examples from both the majority and minority classes enter the sample in the desired proportion. This process is repeated until the algorithm converges. So no information is lost during the optimization process.

Another benefit of this approach is that by increasing the importance weight of the minority class, we give its examples more chance to end up in the most violated constraint and hence, become potential support vectors. This way the imbalanced support-vector ratio is automatically tuned to include more examples from the minority class, which gives more control over the imbalance of classes.

It can be easily shown that the new sampling technique preserves the convergence bounds proven in [16]. Note that drawing examples using rejection sampling (Alg. 2) simply re-weights the original distribution D according to the importance weights of the examples. This means that we are effectively training a cost insensitive classifier under the new transformed distribution $\hat{D}$. By invoking Translation Theorem [17], we establish that, to obtain a cost-sensitive classifier that minimizes the expected risk under the original distribution D, it is sufficient to learn a cost-insensitive classifier under the transformed distribution $\hat{D}$. The CPA that draws examples from D using the sampling scheme in Alg. 2 is equivalent to the original CPA applying uniform sampling to the transformed distribution $\hat{D}$. This allows us to invoke the proof in [16], thus establishing similar convergence bounds.

3.2   Parallelization

The modular nature of the cutting plane algorithm suggests easy parallelization. In fact, in our experiments we observed that at each iteration 95% of the total learning time is spent in the double loop (2), which involves double sum of kernel evaluations over r examples in the sample. This observation suggests high parallelizability of the code. Using p processors the complexity of this predominant part can be brought down from $O(r^2)$ to $O(r^2/p)$.

4   Experimental Evaluation

The goal of our experiments is to study how the problem of imbalanced datasets can be effectively tackled by the new sampling technique that we propose to integrate into the CPA. To do so, we carry out learning on complex text classification tasks where addressing class-imbalance problem plays an important role to obtain the optimal classification performance. In the first set of experiments we compare the accuracy one can get by better parametrizing the model using our proposed method against the cutting plane algorithm with uniform sampling and the conventional SVM. Below we refer to the capability to control the penalty factors for examples from different classes as simply j option (as implemented in SVM-light software). Secondly, we bring the capability of cutting plane algorithm with rejection sampling to alleviate the class-imbalance problem to the large-scale, where training of conventional SVMs soon becomes too time-consuming. We also demonstrate the speedup factors after parallelization. This feature becomes especially appealing nowadays, when shared memory parallel architectures, i.e. multi-processor and multi-core CPUs, are becoming available for general use.

We modified the implementation of the approximate CPA with uniform sampling[16] with SVM-Light-TK[11] to include cost-proportionate sampling strategy. For brevity, we refer to the original CPA with uniform sampling as uSVM, CPA + rejection sampling as uSVM+j, and SVM-light as SVM. In all our experiments we used the subset tree (SST) kernel [2]. For uSVM+j and SVM we report the best results for the optimal value of j parameter that controls Precision/Recall ratio.To measure the classification performance we use Precision, Recall and F_1-score. All the experiments were run on machines equipped with Intel® Xeon® 2.33GHz CPUs carrying 6Gb of RAM under Linux.

We used two different natural language datasets: TREC 10 QA[2] (training: 5,483, test: 500) and Yahoo! Answers (YA)[3] (train: up to 300k, test: 10k) to perform two similar tasks of QA classification. The task for the first dataset is to select the most appropriate type of the answer from a set of given possibilities. The training set consists of 5,483 questions and the test set is composed of 500 questions for each class. The goal of the experiments on these relatively small datasets is to demonstrate that rejection sampling is able to effectively handle class imbalance similar to SVM.

The second corpus is a large subset of Yahoo! Answers dataset. The dataset contains a set of 142,627 non-factoid, i.e. "how to" questions, and 364,419 answers. Testing was carried out on the 10k subset. The classification task was set up as follows. Given pairs of questions and corresponding answers learn if in a given pair the answer is the 'best' answer for a question. The goal of this experiment is to have a large-scale classification task (300k examples in our experiments) to demonstrate that class-imbalance problem can be handled effectively at this scale.

Results on TREC 10 and YA. Experimental results on six different categories of TREC corpus and on YA dataset are reported in Table 1(a) and Table 1(b) respectively. One can see that uSVM algorithm with uniform sampling obtains high precision trying to minimize the training error dominated by examples from negative class and is not able to adjust in the presence of class imbalance. This results in lower values of the recall. On the other hand uSVM+j is able to achieve a better tradeoff between precision and recall resulting in higher F_1 scores. Also the P/R ratio of SVM with the optimal set of parameters suggests that uSVM+j has a better capacity to control the imbalance problem.

(a)

Data	Ratio	uSVM		uSVM+j		SVM	
		F-1	P/R	F-1	P/R	F-1	P/R
ABBR	60:1	87.5	100.0/77.8	84.2	80.0/88.9	84.2	80.0/88.9
DESC	4:1	96.1	95.0/97.1	96.1	95.0/97.1	94.8	97.7/92.0
ENTY	3:1	72.3	91.8/59.6	79.1	79.6/78.7	80.4	82.2/78.7
HUM	3:1	88.1	98.1/80.0	90.3	94.9/86.2	87.5	88.9/86.2
LOC	5:1	81.4	96.6/70.4	87.0	87.5/86.4	82.6	86.5/79.0
NUM	5:1	86.0	98.9/76.1	91.2	96.1/86.7	89.9	98.9/82.3

(b)

10k	1.5:1	37.4	33.5/42.2	39.1	29.6/57.7	37.9	24.2/87.7
50k	2.0:1	36.5	36.0/36.9	40.6	30.0/62.5	39.6	25.7/86.9
100k	2.4:1	33.4	36.2/31.1	40.2	30.2/59.9	40.3	26.6/83.5
150k	2.8:1	33.5	36.9/30.7	41.0	30.2/64.0	-	-
300k	3.4:1	23.8	40.1/16.9	41.4	30.7/63.8	-	-

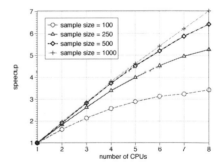

Fig. 1. Results on TREC-10 (a) YA (b) datasets. Ratio - proportion of negative examples with respect to positive; P/R - precision (P) and recall (R).

Fig. 2. Speedups vs number of CPUs after parallelization of CPA on Yahoo! Answers (50k)

[2] http://l2r.cs.uiuc.edu/cogcomp/Data/QA/QC/
[3] retrieved through the Yahoo! Webscope program.

Parallelization. To test the effects of parallelization we carried out experiments on 50,000 subset of YA dataset on 1 to 8 CPUs. The achieved speedups are reported in Fig. 2, where each curve corresponds to training using different sample sizes. Increasing the sample size leads to an increase in the time spent inside the double loop (2), which makes the speedup for larger sample sizes even more significant. Using 8 CPUs gives the speedup factor of about 7.0 using sample size equal to 1000. Since classification can also be easily parallelized it allows one to experiment with larger sample sizes to obtain a more accurate model or carry out training on larger data.

To better demonstrate the advantage of the parallel implementation we replicated the large-scale experiment in [12] on Semantic Role Labeling dataset[4] using 1 million examples. The reported training time was 4 hours for uSVM and 7.5 days for SVM, while our parallel implementation took about 30 minutes for learning on 8 CPUs.

5   Related Work

The most popular method to address class-imbalance problem in SVMs is to introduce cost factors in the primal problem [15]. It is implemented in SVM-light [4] that has a super-linear scaling behavior, which prohibits the experiments on very large datasets.

To improve the scaling properties of SVM-light, a number of CPA-based methods have been proposed (for example, SVM^{perf} [5]). [3] have further improved the convergence rate of the underlying CPA. Another approach to directly optimize for F_1-score, was proposed in [7]. While the aforementioned algorithms deliver fast and accurate solutions, they scale well only when linear kernels are used. Another approach to iteratively extract basis vectors as a part of a cutting plane algorithm is studied in [6]. This, however, leads to a non-trivial optimization problem when arbitrary kernel functions are used.

6   Conclusions

In this paper we proposed a method that combines the benefits of CPA with sampling for training non-linear SVMs on large-scale data together with the flexibility to control the problem of imbalanced data. This improvement becomes particularly significant when learning on large text classification datasets, where class-imbalance plays an important role to obtain the optimal balance between precision and recall. The proposed sampling strategy has shown superior ability to parametrize the model with respect to conventional approach implemented in SVM-light on two Question/Answer classification tasks. We also take advantage of the possibility to parallelize the code to make learning even faster.

The distinctive property of the proposed method is that it directly integrates the cost-proportionate sampling into the CPA optimization process, unlike the

---

[4] `http://danielepighin.net/ cms/research/MixedFeaturesForSRL`

other sampling approaches based on the reductions idea of [17]. In other words, sampling is carried out iteratively, such that no information is discarded from training examples as in "one-shot" sampling methods.

Acknowledgements. This work has been partially supported by the EC project FP247758: Trustworthy Eternal Systems via Evolving Software, Data and Knowledge (EternalS).

References

1. Cancedda, N., Gaussier, E., Goutte, C., Renders, J.M.: Word sequence kernels. Journal of Machine Learning Research 3, 1059–1082 (2003)
2. Collins, M., Duffy, N.: New ranking algorithms for parsing and tagging: Kernels over discrete structures, and the voted perceptron. In: ACL, pp. 263–270 (2002)
3. Franc, V., Sonnenburg, S.: Optimized cutting plane algorithm for support vector machines. In: ICML, pp. 320–327 (2008)
4. Joachims, T.: Making large-scale SVM learning practical. In: Advances in Kernel Methods - Support Vector Learning, ch. 11, pp. 169–184. MIT Press, Cambridge (1999)
5. Joachims, T.: Training linear SVMs in linear time. In: KDD (2006)
6. Joachims, T., Yu, C.N.J.: Sparse kernel svms via cutting-plane training. Machine Learning 76(2-3), 179–193 (2009); European Conference on Machine Learning (ECML) (Special Issue)
7. Joachims, T.: A support vector method for multivariate performance measures. In: ICML, pp. 377–384 (2005)
8. Joachims, T., Finley, T., Yu, C.-N.J.: Cutting-plane training of structural svms. Machine Learning 77(1), 27–59 (2009)
9. Kate, R.J., Mooney, R.J.: Using string-kernels for learning semantic parsers. In: ACL (July 2006)
10. Kudo, T., Matsumoto, Y.: Fast methods for kernel-based text analysis. In: Proceedings of ACL 2003 (2003)
11. Moschitti, A.: Making tree kernels practical for natural language learning. In: EACL. The Association for Computer Linguistics (2006)
12. Severyn, A., Moschitti, A.: Large-Scale Support Vector Learning with Structural Kernels. In: Balcázar, J.L., Bonchi, F., Gionis, A., Sebag, M. (eds.) ECML PKDD 2010. LNCS, vol. 6323, pp. 229–244. Springer, Heidelberg (2010)
13. Shen, L., Sarkar, A., Joshi, A.k.: Using LTAG Based Features in Parse Reranking. In: Proceedings of EMNLP 2006 (2003)
14. Tsochantaridis, I., Joachims, T., Hofmann, T., Altun, Y.: Large margin methods for structured and interdependent output variables. Journal of Machine Learning Research 6, 1453–1484 (2005)
15. Veropoulos, K., Campbell, C., Cristianini, N.: Controlling the sensitivity of support vector machines. In: Proceedings of the International Joint Conference on AI, pp. 55–60 (1999)
16. Yu, C.-N.J., Joachims, T.: Training structural svms with kernels using sampled cuts. In: KDD, pp. 794–802 (2008)
17. Zadrozny, B., Langford, J., Abe, N.: Cost-sensitive learning by cost-proportionate example weighting. In: Proceedings of ICDM (2003)

Combining Machine Learning and Information Retrieval Techniques for Software Clustering

Anna Corazza[1], Sergio Di Martino[1],
Valerio Maggio[1], and Giuseppe Scanniello[2]

[1] University of Naples "Federico II"
{anna.corazza,sergio.dimartino,valerio.maggio}@unina.it
[2] Università della Basilicata, Potenza, Italy
giuseppe.scanniello@unibas.it

Abstract. In the field of Software Maintenance the definition of effective approaches to partition a software system into meaningful subsystems is a longstanding and relevant research topic. These techniques are very important as they can significantly support a Maintainer in his/her tasks by grouping related entities of a large system into smaller and easier to comprehend subsystems.

In this paper we investigate the effectiveness of combining information retrieval and machine learning techniques in order to exploit the lexical information provided by programmers for software clustering. In particular, differently from any related work, we employ indexing techniques to explore the contribution of the combined use of six different dictionaries, corresponding to the six parts of the source code where programmers introduce lexical information, namely: class, attribute, method and parameter names, comments, and source code statements. Moreover their relevance is estimated on the basis of the project characteristics, by applying a machine learning approach based on a probabilistic model and on the Expectation-Maximization algorithm. To group source files accordingly, two clustering algorithms have been compared, i.e. the K-Medoids and the Group Average Agglomerative Clustering, and the investigation has been conducted on a dataset of 9 open source Java software systems.

Keywords: Expectation-Maximization algorithm, Information Retrieval, Probabilistic Model, Remodularization, Software Clustering, Software Evolution.

1 Introduction

One of the most demanding activities of the maintenance process is the Program Comprehension. It can take up to 60% of the total maintenance effort [18]. The main reasons are: (I) some pieces of knowledge on the specific domain covered by the application to maintain are not explicitly stated in the documentation [16]; (II) the documentation is missing or not up-to-date. In order to support a software Maintainer, source files which are in some way related could be grouped together into clusters, thus being easier to comprehend [35].

A. Moschitti and R. Scandariato (Eds.): EternalS 2011, CCIS 255, pp. 42–60, 2012.

Many research efforts have been devoted to address this issue. A number of these approaches generally attempt to discover clusters by analyzing structural dependencies between software artifacts [2, 3, 36]. However, if the analysis is based on the sole structural aspect, a key source of information about the analyzed software system may be lost, i.e. the domain knowledge that developers embed by means of code comments, names of methods, classes, and identifiers. As a consequence, some efforts are being devoted to investigate the use of lexical information for software clustering [6, 16, 20, 29].

In this paper, we describe an approach towards software clustering, falling in the lexical-based group. The main contribution of the proposal is in the way we exploit this lexical information. Indeed, all the similar approaches treat all the terms in the source code as equally important. This means, for example, that a term coming from a comment is considered as informative as a term in a class name. However, in our opinion, developers may place different care in choosing words for the various code elements (class names, attribute names, comments, etc...), and then the associated relevance in the conveyed information may be different.

As a consequence, we investigated the effects of considering separately the contribution of six vocabularies, composed of terms extracted by the different parts, or *zones*, where a programmer can add lexical information, namely: (I) *Class Names*, (II) *Attribute Names*, (III) *Method Names*, (IV) *Parameter Names* (V) *Comments* and (VI) *Source Code Statements*. Thanks to this separation, we applied an automatic weighting mechanism to exploit the contribution of each vocabulary. Since each software system has its own development peculiarities, no general weighting schema can be defined, but rather it should be suited for each specific system at the hand.

To this aim, we introduced a *probabilistic model* of the data, whose parameters, including the zone weights, are optimized by means of an iterative algorithm, namely the *Expectation-Maximization* (EM) [24]. Then, these automatically computed weights have been used as multipliers in a *Vector Space Model* representation [22] of the software system, useful to compute similarity among classes.

Finally, once given this similarity, to group software entities we compared the results of two well-known clustering algorithms, namely *K-Medoids* [14], and *Group Average Agglomerative Clustering* (GAAC) [22] which we have properly customized to make them more suitable for the software clustering domain.

To evaluate whether the introduction of the probabilistic model as well as the use of different clustering algorithms improved the resulting partitions, the approach has been assessed in a case study. Since no "gold-standard" partition is available in the software clustering domain [35], we selected 9 well-known open source software systems implemented in Java and we assessed whether the proposed approach was able to automatically group classes in a fashion resembling an authoritative partition, i.e. the original partition of the system (intended as classes in packages) defined for these systems, as done in other works (e.g.: [4, 29, 37]).

The results we got indicate that the introduction of the probabilistic model highly enhances the process, leading to clusters significantly more similar to the authoritative partitions. With respect to such improvement in the design of input features the choice of the clustering algorithm showed to have a much smaller effect on performance.

2   Related Works

The most expensive activity in the software life cycle is the maintenance [18]. It starts after the delivery of the first version and ends when the system is discarded. The costs concerning the software maintenance decrease in case the software architecture documentation is properly managed and updated. Unfortunately, the common practice in the software industry is far from consistently maintaining documentation with the changes made to the source code [5, 11]. In this typical scenario, the partitioning of a software system into small and easier to comprehend subsystems represents a longstanding and relevant research topic [1–3, 36].

The greater part of of the proposed approaches generate clusters by analyzing only the structural dependencies between software entities [2, 3, 8, 21, 23, 26, 36]. More recently a number of techniques have been proposed that exploit lexical information provide by developers within source code [6, 16, 20, 30].

In particular, Kuhn *et al.* in [16] describe a language independent approach to group software artifacts based on Latent Semantic Indexing (LSI) [9]. This approach tries to group source code containing similar terms in the comments and is implemented on top of the Moose re-engineering environment [28]. Linguistic topics are also associated to each cluster of a given partition of documents (e.g., classes or methods). To identify how the clusters are related to each other a correlation matrix is used. The authors perform a qualitative analysis of the clustering results, while no quantitative analysis is executed. Our approach is different as we introduce the concept of the zones where to mine information extracted from source code and we automatically weight them using a probabilistic model.

Furthermore, Scanniello *et al.* [30] present an approach to automate the software system partitioning. This approach first analyzes the software entities (e.g., programs or classes) and uses LSI to get the dissimilarity between the entities, which are grouped using iteratively the K-Means clustering algorithm. To assess the validity of the approach a case study on open source software systems has been conducted. The main difference with respect to the approach presented here is that there is no distinction among the zone where lexical information is gathered.

Similarly to the present work, many are the comparative studies among different clustering algorithms proposed in literature. Wiggerts [36] analyzes the clustering algorithms commonly used to group software entities and provides a theoretical background for applying them in the software remodularization. An extension of this work is presented by Anquetil and Lethbridge in [3]. In particular, they present a comparative study of different hierarchical clustering algorithms and analyze their properties with respect to the remodularization of software systems. Similarly, Maqbool and Babri in [23] highlight hierarchical clustering research in the context of software architecture recovery and remodularization. The main contribution of their work is the analysis of two clustering based approaches and their experimental assessment on some large software systems. Also, Tzerpos and Holt in [32] study a number of software clustering algorithms and compare their performance. The comparison is conducted generating randomly "perturbed" versions of an example system. Differences between the partition identified by the clustering algorithms and the original partition of the system are measured by using the MoJo distance [31], that will be described in Section 4.

Wu *et al.* in [37] present a comparative study of four clustering algorithms: two agglomerative clustering algorithms based on the Jaccard coefficient and on the complete and the single linkage update rules respectively; an algorithm based on program comprehension patterns to recover subsystems that are commonly found in manually-created decompositions of large software systems; and a customized configuration of an algorithm implemented in Bunch [21]. Five large C/C++ open source systems are used to compare the performance of these algorithms. In particular, the performance is analyzed with respect to the authoritativeness of the identified clusters (using the MoJo) and the non-extremity of distribution of the size of these clusters using the NED (Non-Extreme Distribution). Similarly, in [4] an empirical study is presented to evaluate four different clustering algorithms, namely (I) Edge betweenness clustering, (II) K-Means clustering, (III) modularization quality clustering, and (IV) design structure matrix clustering, in a case study of four Java systems. Differently from [37], the authoritativeness of the clustering results is computed by using the MoJoSim, a normalized version of MoJo [34], also described in Section 4, that is the measure employed in the assessment of this work.

3   The Proposed Approach to Cluster Software Systems

The definition of our software clustering approach encompasses the following three steps: (I) the identification of a proper set of features based on the different parts occurring in each software entity (Section 3.1); (II) the definition of a probabilistic model able to account for the different relevance of such zones with an *a-priori* probability (Section 3.2) and (III) the use of a clustering algorithm properly suited for the specific domain (Section 3.3).

3.1   Feature Extraction and Zones

The first task towards the definition of our software clustering approach regards the definition of a technique that is able to extract the lexical information from the source code and to organize it into some meaningful structures, suitable for further processing. Since we are interested in the processing of lexical information, we assume that each source file can be treated as a common plain-text document to which text mining and information retrieval (IR) techniques are applied. Therefore we start by considering the *class* as the *document unit* [22], namely the granularity at which each processed source file must be segmented. Then, for each document (class), we collect the lexical information provided in the six zones of code considered in [6], namely Class Names *(CN)*, Attribute Names *(AN)*, Function Names *(FN)*, Parameter Names *(PN)*, Comments *(Co)* and Source Code Statements *(SCS)*. These zones represent the six different parts into which a developer can add lexical information. Therefore, in our approach, the content of each document is defined by the combination of six different *vocabularies* of terms, one for each zones. In particular the *CN* zone contains the name of the class associated to the document together with terms occurring in class annotations. The *AN* zone contains the names of attributes and constants of the class while the *FN* and *PN* zones contain respectively the words occurring in method names and annotations, and those contained in the names of parameters (and their types in case they are not primitive). The fifth and the sixth zones, namely the *Co* and the *SCS* zones, contain all the terms extracted from comments and from the body of methods, such as the names of local variables, passed parameters, etc.... As for the fifth zone, it is worth noting that if the source file starts with a copyright disclaimer as a beginning comment, we removed it since it does not convey any useful information.

Once all the documents have been collected and all their vocabularies have been gathered, the next step is to construct a *dictionary*[22] defined by the union of all these vocabularies. As a consequence, the resulting dictionary collects all the terms appearing in at least one document. Although the dictionary construction is similar to the one employed on natural language text, it has some specificities connected to the fact that it works on text extracted from source code. First of all, there is to tackle the problem that usually identifiers are made of many concatenated words. Thus, we remove all punctuations characters and numbers, and then we tokenize the identifiers according to various naming conventions. In particular we handle the use of *Camel-case* (capitalized letters used to divide words) and of underscores as word separators. Afterwards we lowercase all the terms, and then remove all the ones appearing in a list of common terms, known as *stop words* (e.g.: the, a, is, etc...) as these terms do not provide any useful information for the analysis. To take into account the peculiarities of the considered domain, we apply different *stop words* lists to the six different zones. In particular, we remove the most common English terms[1] occurring from the first four zones. As for the fifth and sixth zones, we remove also all the keywords of the programming language. Then, all the remaining terms are gathered in *equivalence classes* according to their morphological root or *stem*. Finally, following an approach widely adopted by information retrieval systems, we represent our documents by the *bag-of-words* model [22]. This model regards each document as a collection of words whose orders and positions are completely disregarded. Indeed, in our approach, we slightly modified the latter assumption as we are interested to the particular zone of the document in which each terms

---

[1] http://www.textfixer.com/resources/common-english-words.txt

occur. Thus if the same term appears in two different zones, it is handled as two distinct terms. Within the *bag-of-words* model, each document is represented by an array of real numbers, where each element is associated to the corresponding term in the *dictionary*. From a different point of view, this is equivalent to considering each document as a point in a multi-dimensional geometrical space: the so-called *vector space model*. In more details, for each term of the dictionary and for each document, the *tf-idf* score is computed. It is defined as follows: given a collection of N documents, namely the number of classes of the system under investigation, the $\mathrm{tf}(t, d)$ (*term frequency*) is defined as the number of occurrences of the term t in the document d. The $\mathrm{idf}(t)$ (*inverse document frequency*) is given by $\log \frac{N}{df(t)}$, where $df(t)$ (*document frequency*) returns the number of documents in which the term t occurs. Finally the *tf-idf* is then defined on the pair (t, d) by

$$\text{tf-idf}(t, d) = \mathrm{tf}(t, d) \cdot \log \frac{N}{\mathrm{df}(t)} \tag{1}$$

The *tf-idf* scoring is adopted in a large number of information retrieval applications because of the good compromise between simplicity and effectiveness in describing the relevance of the term with respect to the document. In fact, its corresponding value increases with the number of occurrences of the term in the document and decreases with the number of documents in which the term appears. Note that the inverse correlation with the document frequency has the effect of lowering the score for terms appearing in all or nearly all documents. The rationale underlying the *idf* is that, when computing similarity among documents as during the clustering process, if a term belongs to all documents, then its discriminative contribution is irrelevant. In this case, its $df = N$, and its *idf* is zero as the its *tf-idf*. Conversely, *idf* augments when the number of documents in which the term appears decreases and attains its maximum ($\log N$) when the term occurs in a unique document.

Concluding, each document is therefore represented by a vector having size equal to the dictionary size, where each element corresponds to the *tf-idf* score for the term in the document. For all the terms not belonging to the document, the corresponding element in the vector is zero.

3.2   Probabilistic Model

In this approach, we investigate the conjecture that the considered zones of the code could convey information of different relevance starting from the observation that developers may place different care in writing code as well as comments. Therefore, the informative contribution of the different zones should be correctly weighted to best exploit the conveyed information. Moreover since these weights strongly depend on the specificities of each project, their choice can not be made subjectively, but should be automatically estimated from the data. To this aim we define an automatic technique that is able to estimate such "relevance" on the basis of the lexical characteristics of each considered project. In particular, we are interested in determining the weights of the zones to be used as multiplicative factors for the *tf-idf* values of the terms during the similarity computation among documents.

A well founded framework to solve such a problem is given by probabilistic approaches, where different sources of information are combined by an *a-priori* probability distribution. The *Maximum Likelihood Estimation* (MLE) is one of the most widely adopted approaches to estimate parameters of a probabilistic model. This approach aims at finding the parameters of the considered model which maximize the probability of the set of samples. In other words, we ought to maximize the probability assigned by the model to all the documents in the project.

If we look at the Z zones (six in our case) as a partition of documents, the probability of each document is given by the product of the joint probabilities of the zones, assuming that the *tf-idf* values of the terms in each of them are produced by a random variable having a Gaussian distribution. In such a model, the probability of a document d_i is defined as follows:

$$P(d_i) = \prod_{z=1}^{Z} P(d_i, z_i) = \prod_{z=1}^{Z} \lambda_z \mathcal{G}(\mu_z, \sigma_z) \tag{2}$$

Thus, our probabilistic model is expressed by a mixtures of multivariate Gaussian distributions, combined by the a-priori probability of each zone, namely λ_z. Our goal consists in finding the parameters λ_z, μ_z and σ_z that maximize the (Log) Likelihood of the project:

$$\text{logL} = \sum_{i=1}^{N} \log \sum_{z=1}^{Z} \lambda_z \mathcal{G}(\mu_z, \sigma_z) \tag{3}$$

However, such parameters can not be found directly because the probability of each document depends on all the considered Gaussians: whenever one of the priors increases, the resulting logLikelihood could also increase. On the other hand, if we know the values of each prior, we are able to find the values of the other parameters. In this conditions, the Expectation - Maximization (EM) algorithm [10] is probably the most largely used choice.

EM is an iterative algorithm whose name refers to the corresponding two main steps it alternates during the execution: in the *Expectation* step, the weights corresponding to each pair (*document*, *zone*) are (re)computed on the basis of the parameters values. On the other hand, the *Maximization* step (re)computes the model parameters in a way that the likelihood does not decrease. The algorithm halts when the increase in likelihood corresponding to a given iteration is smaller than a given threshold, or when a maximum number of iterations has been performed.

Finally, among all the resulting parameters, the algorithm returns the values of the zone priors: a large value of λ_z suggests that the z-th zone contribution is important for the model. Therefore, we want to combine the zone scores with weights proportional to these priors. As both weights and priors ought to sum to one, we choose priors exactly equal to weights.

However, it is worth noting that one of the problems of the EM algorithm is that it can attain a local maximum rather than a global one. Therefore, the choice of the initial values for the parameters is very critical for the optimization results [25]. To this aim, two different initialization strategies have been experimentally compared. In particular the first strategy (we named *random*) chooses the initial weights randomly (EM_{Rnd}), while the second one (we named *frequentist*) estimates them by the rate between the number of tokens in the zones and the total number of tokens (EM_{Freq}). The idea underlying the latter choice is that it assigns more importance to regions containing more lexical information.

3.3   Clustering

The Software Clustering problem, within the Software Maintenance field, can be defined as the clustering of related software entities. Even if this definition is quite simplistic, it points out the fact that this problem has a lot of aspects in common with typical clustering tasks. First of all, it belongs to the category of *hard clustering* tasks in which all the entities, namely the classes of the system in our case, can be associated to only one cluster. Moreover, as any other *unsupervised* machine learning approach, one of the key issues of the technique is the choice of the similarity measure, which is crucial for the clustering performance since it states criteria to decide whether two software entities are similar enough to be put into the same cluster. In the defined vector space model, the similarity between two classes could be estimated by means of the *cosine similarity*[22], expressed as the cosine of the angle determined by the two vectors representing them. In addition to that, clustering of software entities introduces some constraints imposed by the specific domain. The most important one is that an automatically produced partition should not be either too huge (i.e. containing hundreds of software entities) nor too tiny (i.e. containing very few software entities) [37].

For this reason, standard algorithms may not be effective unless they are modified to impose such constraints. Therefore in this paper we discuss how two well-known clustering algorithms, namely the *K-Medoids* (Section 3.4) and the *Group Average Agglomerative Clustering* (Section 3.5), that have been slightly customized to be more suitable to the specificity of software clustering tasks.

3.4   K-Medoids

The K-Medoids is a clustering algorithm similar to the classical K-Means [14], except that each cluster is built around a really existing entity of the dataset, namely the *medoid*, rather than around the mean of the cluster elements, which could correspond to no actual element. This aspect has the effect to make the algorithm more robust with respect to outliers. Moreover, since the resulting clustering strongly depends on the initial choice of medoids, which is random, to avoid that such randomness leads to unbalanced solutions, we introduced a novel halting criterion to avoid the risk of resulting in extremely small or extremely large clusters, which makes sense in the context of Software Clustering.

Indeed, the original K-Medoids algorithm starts with a random choice of the k medoids and iterates assigning at each step all the entities to the most similar medoids, and then recomputing the medoids. Finally the algorithm returns the desired partitions of the system organized as a set of k different clusters. However, the main drawback of the algorithm is that resulting clusters strongly depends on the initial configurations. Thus, unlucky configurations could result in a partition including too small clusters: in the variant of the algorithm proposed in [7], the whole procedure is repeated until a final solution with no extreme clusters is attained or a maximum number of iterations are performed. Even when the procedure halts due to the latter condition, the algorithm provides the best solution among all the ones found in each iteration.

3.5   Group Average Agglomerative Clustering

In addition to the K-Medoids algorithm, we considered also the Group Average Agglomerative Clustering (GAAC) [22].

This algorithm belongs to the category of the so-called Hierarchical Agglomerative Clustering (HAC) [27] that *agglomerates* all the clusters according to a Bottom-Up strategy. In particular, the algorithm starts by treating each entity as a singleton cluster, and then iteratively merges the most similar pairs of clusters, until all the clusters have been merged [13]. The resulting hierarchy of clusters is visualized as a *dendrogram* in which leaf nodes represent singletons and each horizontal line corresponds to a merge between two clusters.

The core of each HAC algorithm is represented by the *linkage phase* which is responsible to determine the pair of clusters to be merged at each iteration. Indeed, different linkage strategies correspond to different HAC algorithms and their choice is crucial as for the properties of resulting clusters [22]. In our approach, we employ the *Group Average Linkage* method that agglomerates two clusters based on the the average similarity of all pairs of entities belonging to them. This strategy has the main advantages of being more robust with respect to outliers and tends to produce more balanced dendrograms [22].

The main feature of this clustering algorithm is that it is deterministic and does not require several random initialization as the K-Medoids. Moreover, although the asymptotic time complexity of the HAC approach is worse than the K-medoids, in the experiments we performed the K-medoids was slower because it was applied a large number of times on different initial points.

Conversely, from a software clustering point of view, the main drawback of the HAC is that it does not provide a flat partition of the system due to its agglomerative nature, but to get these partitions of the classes, the dendrogram has to be properly cut. Therefore in [6] we defined a cutting strategy criterion that optimizes the non extremity distribution of the partition aiming to generate at most k clusters in order to make the two clustering strategies comparable.

4   Experimental Assessment

The potentiality of the approach as been experimentally assessed, with special attention to the clustering algorithm contribution. Also the choice of the EM initialization strategy, either random or frequentist, has been part of the empirical investigation. Since the trend effect should be independent of the clustering algorithm, we only considered the GAAC in this experiment. Therefore, the first issue we consider in this section is the choice of a suitable clustering performance measure. A brief description of the employed data sets follows, while Section 5 is devoted to the discussion of the assessment results.

4.1   Measures

The assessment of a clustering is usually based on an annotated test set, usually referred as *gold standard*, in which each item of the dataset is labeled with the corresponding cluster. In case of software clustering tasks, this gold standard could be represented by a set of large and publicly available software systems with well-understood decomposition that can be used as benchmark [35]. However, from one hand, there is no publicly annotated dataset available; on the other hand, the manual generation of such partitions by software architects may be too subjective to represent a benchmark.

Therefore, following other similar works [4, 6, 29, 37], we adopted a fair and repeatable procedure for constructing the gold case clustering which is built on the original source folder structure of the system under investigation. The idea behind this protocol is the following: given the bunch of classes of a well-engineered system (such as for instance *JHotDraw*, widely used to teach Software Design issues) without any structure, if the approach is able to automatically arrange them in a partitioning that resembles the packages proposed by the developers of the system, then the approach will likely perform well also on other software systems. From the software engineering point of view, this measure is called *Authoritativeness (Auth)* [37].

The *authoritative partition* is automatically derived in accordance with the following three steps:

1. create the subsystem hierarchy based on the directory (package) structure (each directory represents a single subsystem);
2. merge a subsystem with its parent if it contains less than five source files;
3. create a cluster for each resulting subsystem.

Given such authoritative partition, the next challenge is to determine a measure that is able to compare clustering results to this partition. Several researchers in literature have attempted to tackle this problem [3, 15, 17, 34].

One of the first proposed approach was the measure presented by Lakhotia and Gravely [17]. However this measure could be used only on dendrograms of hierarchical clusterings which in practice strongly limits its applicability to other not-hierarchical clustering algorithms.

Afterwards Anquetil and Lethbridge proposed the use of the well known measures of *Precision* and *Recall* for the evaluation of clustering results [3]. In particular, let A be the automatically identified source partition and B the authoritative partition, they defined the Precision as the percentage of intra-pairs, i.e. pairs of items in the same cluster, in A that are also intra-pairs in B. On the other hand, the Recall is defined as the percentage of intra-pairs in B that are also intra-pairs in A. The main drawback of this measure is that it is too much "sensitive" to the number and the size of considered clusters. As a consequence, few misplaced entities in a cluster could produce very different results.

Koschke and Eisenbarth presented in [15] a complex measure which extends and removes limitations of the approach proposed by Lakhotia and Gravely and that is loosely based on the Precision and Recall measures employed by Anquetil and Lethbridge. The KE measure is built on the definition of $GOOD$ and OK matches. Assuming that p is a threshold parameter and that A_i and B_j are two clusters in the source and authoritative partition respectively, the following two definitions hold:

$$(\text{GOOD match}) \; A_i \approx_p B_j \, iff \frac{|A_i \cap B_j|}{|A_i \cup B_j|} \geq p$$

$$(\text{OK match}) \; A_i \subseteq_p B_j \, iff \frac{|A_i \cap B_j|}{|A_i|} \geq p$$

These two matching definitions are then used to split the set of clusters in two distinct classes, one for each relationship. Next, once all the clusters have been classified, the GOOD class is enlarged by joining all the OK matches in which one of the two cluster is already in the GOOD class. All the remaining clusters that are neither in GOOD or in OK matches are referred as *false positives* or *true negatives* in case they belong to the source or to the authoritative partition, respectively.

Finally the overall similarity metric is defined as follows:

$$KE(A,B) = \frac{\displaystyle\sum_{(a,b)\in GOOD} \frac{|a \cap b|}{|a \cup b|} + \sum_{(a,b)\in OK} \frac{|a \cap b|}{|a \cup b|}}{|GOOD| + |OK| + |truenegatives|}$$

The KE metric is particularly good when the source partition is close to the authoritative partition. Conversely it is not as good in more extreme cases as its definition takes into account only the union and the intersection between clusters, without applying any penalty for the join operations. Last but not least, it relies on the specification of a threshold parameter which could inevitably bias the results.

More recently, Tzerpos and Holt presented in [31] the *MoJo* distance, which is the measure this work builds on. In particular, let A be the automatically identified source partition and B the authoritative partition, $MoJo(A, B)$ is defined as:

$$\text{MoJo(A, B)} = \min(\text{mno}(A, B), \text{mno}(B, A))$$

corresponding to the minimum number of *Move* and *Join* operations necessary to transform either the first partition A to the second partition B or vice versa [31]. The lower the value of MoJo between two partitions is, the more the clustering algorithm is effective in creating the software partition.

Differently from the *KE* measure, this metric explicitly introduce the calculation of a penalty to the join operations but it has a couple of drawbacks that make its original formulation useless for the assessment of our approach. First of all we are interested in determining how the automatically defined partition resembles the authoritative one and not vice versa. Thus we need to calculate only the $mno(A, B)$. Furthermore, the measure does not make the results comparable among different software systems as its value strongly depend on the size of their authoritative partitions.

Therefore, to overcome those limitations, we used a normalized version of *MoJo*, namely the *MoJoSim* [4] defined as follows:

$$\text{MoJoSim(A, B)} = 1 - \frac{\text{mno}(A, B)}{N} \qquad (4)$$

where N is the number of entities of the software system to be clustered.

In conclusion, the Auth measure gives an estimate of the similarity between the clustering proposed by our approach and those in an authoritative partition. However, this aspect is not sufficient to evaluate the quality of the solution. Indeed, we also require that the obtained clustering does not include too small or too large clusters. To this aim, a measure called *Non-extremity cluster distribution (NED)* has been introduced by [37]. NED is defined as follows:

$$NED = \frac{1}{N} \sum_{c_i \in C: \text{MinSize} \le |c_i| \le \text{MaxSize}} |c_i|$$

where N is the number of classes of the analyzed software system and C represents the set of clusters. In accordance to other similar researches, we limited cluster size to be included between MinSize= 5 and MaxSize= 100. In other words, clusters with less than 5 or more than 100 software entities are considered as extreme lower and upper limits, respectively [37]. The larger the NED value is, the more non-extreme the size distribution of the clusters is.

4.2   Data Sets

For the evaluation of the proposed approach we used a dataset with the following nine Java projects:

- **EasyMock** is a tool for Test-Driven Development. It provides Mock Objects for interfaces by generating them on the fly using Java proxy mechanism.
- **JabRef** is an open source bibliography reference manager.
- **JHotDraw** is a GUI framework for technical and structured graphics.
- **JFreeChart** is a tool supporting the visualization of bar charts, pie charts, line charts, scatter plots, histograms, simple Gantt charts,bubble plots, and more.

- **PMD** is a Java source code analyzer. It finds unused variables, empty catch blocks, unnecessary object creation, and so forth.
- **FindBugs** is a system that uses static analysis to look for bugs in Java code.
- **ArgoUML** is an open source UML modeling tool that includes support for all standard UML 1.4 diagrams.
- **EclipseJdt** is the Java infrastructure of the Java Editor included in Eclipse IDE.
- **JdkSwing** is the primary Java GUI widget toolkit that provides an API for creating and manipulating graphical user interfaces for Java programs.

All these software systems can be freely downloaded from SourceForge [2]. Some descriptive statistics of these systems are shown in Table 1. In particular, this table shows names of the software systems and the analyzed versions. The third column shows the number of classes, together with the number of thousand of lines of code (KLOCs) and thousands of lines of comments (KCLOCs) of each considered software reported in the last two columns.

Table 1. Descriptive statistics of the authoritative partitions

System	Version	Classes	KLOCs	KCLOCs
EasyMock	2.4	65	4.16	1.9
JabRef	2.4B2	1082	75.19	21.31
JHotDraw	7.4.1	953	86.13	35.84
JFreeChart	1.0.13	610	122.58	107.6
PMD	4.2.5	702	59.38	9.42
FindBugs	1.3.9	243	13.06	3.26
ArgoUML	0.3.2	1928	161.43	117.67
EclipseJdt	3.2	341	55.30	65.64
JdkSwing	1.4.0	1552	115.37	102.35

5   Results and Discussion

The assessment is based on the two measures introduced in Section 4.1, namely Auth and NED. However, their role in the discussion of the assessment results is different. From one hand, the Auth provides an indication of the external "quality" of the clusters identified by the approach. On the other hand, the NED provides an indication of the internal quality of the resulting partition of the system. As a consequence, even if we aim at the definition of clustering strategies obtaining acceptable NED values, larger NED does not always imply that the clustering is better.

To this aim, although we always report both Auth and NED, we mainly discuss the Auth trend, while we evaluate NED values only to control that the constructed partition fulfills the non extremity requirement.

---

[2] http://sourceforge.net

The first issue considered by the experimental assessment regards the choice of the initialization strategy in the EM algorithm. Indeed, as discussed in Section 3 two strategies are possible: the initial parameters can be either randomly set or estimated by the frequency of the corresponding event. A disadvantage of the former strategy is that the final results are not deterministic and the algorithm ought to be run a number of times to eventually choose the best likelihood maximum and this obviously affect the approach computational complexity.

Table 2. Authoritativeness and NED Values for the different EM initialization strategies using GAAC

System	Authoritativeness		NED	
	EM_{Rnd}	EM_{Freq}	EM_{Rnd}	EM_{Freq}
EasyMock	0.725	0.815	0.701	0.792
JabRef	0.668	0.749	0.921	0.981
JHotDraw	0.544	0.757	0.951	0.978
JFreeChart	0.47	0.57	0.988	0.992
PMD	0.475	0.595	0.915	0.989
FindBugs	0.877	0.877	0.923	0.947
ArgoUML	0.521	0.711	0.959	0.987
EclipseJdt	0.731	0.765	0.909	0.962
JdkSwing	0.732	0.762	0.933	0.992

Experimental results for the comparison of the two strategies are presented in Table 2 from which it clearly results that with no exception frequentist initialization performs better than the random one for both Auth and NED. This has also a good impact on computational complexity.

Furthermore, we assumed that the choice of the EM initialization should be independent from the rest of the system pipeline, including the clustering algorithm. This hypothesis is confirmed by the experimental results comparing the effect of the EM introduction on the two clustering algorithms we are considering, namely GAAC and K-Medoids, presented in Table 3. Indeed, as better discussed in the following, GAAC nearly always works better than K-Medoids, both with and without the EM algorithm.

Tables 3 and 4 report the performance obtained for the two clustering algorithms both with and without EM. Auth is nearly always larger for GAAC, independently on whether the input representation considers the EM or not. When considering the baseline without EM, the only project on which K-Medoids performs better is the EclipseJdt software system. Also in this case, however, Auth values obtained by the two clustering algorithms are very close. The same trend in the results still holds in case both the zones and EM are introduced. In particular the K-Medoids performs better only for the ArgoUML software systems, while in all other cases, the Auth values obtained by GAAC are always better than the ones obtained by K-Medoids.

Table 3. Authoritativeness for GAAC and K-Medoids Clustering with and without the use of EM

| System | Authoritativeness | | | |
| | GAAC | | K-Medoids | |
	NO-EM	EM_{Freq}	NO-EM	EM_{Freq}
EasyMock	0.631	0.815	0.572	0.812
JabRef	0.589	0.749	0.392	0.735
JHotDraw	0.361	0.757	0.257	0.753
JFreeChart	0.402	0.570	0.361	0.577
PMD	0.373	0.595	0.325	0.571
FindBugs	0.840	0.877	0.790	0.874
ArgoUML	0.376	0.711	0.331	0.659
EclipseJdt	0.551	0.765	0.574	0.742
JdkSwing	0.601	0.762	0.399	0.737

Table 4. NED for GAAC and K-Medoids Clustering with and without the use of EM

| System | NED | | | |
| | GAAC | | K-Medoids | |
	NO-EM	EM_{Freq}	NO-EM	EM_{Freq}
EasyMock	0.938	0.792	0.998	0.920
JabRef	0.986	0.981	0.501	0.496
JHotDraw	0.980	0.978	0.752	0.751
JFreeChart	0.980	0.992	0.918	0.924
PMD	0.986	0.989	0.571	0.524
FindBugs	0.947	0.947	0.342	0.351
ArgoUML	0.994	0.987	0.809	0.801
EclipseJdt	0.962	0.962	0.890	0.881
JdkSwing	0.983	0.992	0.618	0.609

As for the NED values, all the achieved results are always acceptable but this was quite expected as we modified the two algorithms in order to respect the requirement on the size of resulting clusters.

Last but not least, the most evident conclusion we can draw from the experimental assessment is that the introduction of zones with weights estimated by EM on a probabilistic model always heavily improves performance. Indeed, the boost introduced is often very relevant. We judge this result very encouraging, showing how approaches taken from information retrieval and machine learning can be adapted and successfully applied to the mining of software repositories.

6   Conclusions

A common scenario that has to be faced during the maintenance of a software system is the lack of reliable documentation, that often is missing or not properly up-to-date. In this situation, reverse engineering tools have to be employed to align it with the actual implemented software architecture [1, 23, 33]. These tools usually rely on clustering-based approaches to group sets of related classes, exploiting some structural-based measures of similarity among software artifacts.

In this paper we have investigated the use of a similarity measure based on lexical information for clustering related software artifacts. In particular, we have explored the effects of mining the lexical information as if they come from six different vocabularies: *Class Names*, *Attributes Names*, *Function Names*, *Parameter Names*, *Comments*, and *Source Code Statements*.

However we investigate the hypothesis that each project has its own peculiarities as for the distribution and the relevance of the terms within these zones. Thus, to exploit at its best the potentials of the lexical information embedded in a software system, a mechanism to automatically weight the importance of each vocabulary is absolutely required.

To this aim, we used the Expectation-Maximization algorithm in order to maximize the (Log)Likelihood of the data according to a probabilistic model of the data defined on the basis of the characteristics of each analyzed software system. Moreover, as the choice of the initial values of the model parameters is a key issue, we explored two different initialization strategies based on a random choice and on the frequencies of the terms within the zones.

The results of the clustering on these features have been then evaluated using two criteria: Authoritativeness and Non-Extremity Distribution (NED). These have been applied on 9 open source Java systems.

The first key finding we got is that the introduction of a weighting technique highly improves results, with a mean enhancement of 40% in terms of authoritativeness, on the considered dataset. Moreover we got the empirical evidence that the frequency based initialization strategy for the EM algorithm always led to better results with respect to a random initialization.

Finally, to understand whether the introduction of the EM and of the probabilistic model always improve the achieved results, regardless the choice of the particular clustering strategy, we compared the performance of two different algorithms, i.e. the K-Medoids and the Group Average Agglomerative Clustering (GAAC).

Even if the latter provided nearly worse results in terms of NED if compared with the results we got with the K-Medoids, GAAC has the great point of strength of being deterministic, so each time a Maintainer will run the whole approach, he/she will get the same clusters. Moreover, we got the empirical evidence that results are largely comparable in terms of Authoritativeness.

Several are the possible future direction for our work. A first direction could be the investigation of software systems implemented in different object oriented programming languages. Moreover, we will investigate the use of commercial software systems, rather than open source ones. At the same time, it will be very interesting to investigate the possibility to infer potential relationships between the relevance of each zone, and some process-specific elements, such as the adopted development methodology. We also plan to investigate the possibility of extending the preprocessing phase using an approach to recognize words from abbreviated identifiers, such as [12], [19], and to automatically associate labels to the clusters. In addition to that, it will very interesting to investigate if different probabilistic model defined on the data would lead to different results. In particular, instead of considering the values of the *tf-idf* of terms as associated to a random variable that follows a Guassian distribution, we should explore different distributions such as the Multinomial or the Bernoulli distributions. Finally, the possibility of merging lexical information with the structural one, coming from the original structure of the classes within the packages will be investigated.

References

1. Andreopoulos, B., An, A., Tzerpos, V., Wang, X.: Clustering large software systems at multiple layers. Information & Software Technology 49(3), 244–254 (2007)
2. Andritsos, P., Tzerpos, V.: Information-theoretic software clustering. IEEE Trans. Software Eng. 31(2), 150–165 (2005)
3. Anquetil, N., Fourrier, C., Lethbridge, T.C.: Experiments with clustering as a software remodularization method. In: WCRE 1999: Proceedings of the Sixth Working Conference on Reverse Engineering, p. 235. IEEE Computer Society, Washington, DC (1999)
4. Bittencourt, R.A., Guerrero, D.D.S.: Comparison of graph clustering algorithms for recovering software architecture module views. In: CSMR 2009: Proceedings of the 2009 European Conference on Software Maintenance and Reengineering, pp. 251–254. IEEE Computer Society, Washington, DC (2009)
5. Bowman, I.T., Holt, R.C., Brewster, N.V.: Linux as a case study: its extracted software architecture. In: ICSE 1999: Proceedings of the 21st International Conference on Software Engineering, pp. 555–563. ACM, New York (1999)
6. Corazza, A., Di Martino, S., Maggio, V., Scanniello, G.: Investigating the use of lexical information for software system clustering. In: 15th European Conference on Software Maintenance and Reengineering (CSMR 2011), pp. 35–44 (2011)
7. Corazza, A., Di Martino, S., Scanniello, G.: A probabilistic based approach towards software system clustering. In: 14th European Conference on Software Maintenance and Reengineering (CSMR 2010), pp. 89–98 (2010)
8. De Lucia, A., Scanniello, G., Tortora, G.: Identifying similar pages in web applications using a competitive clustering algorithm: Special issue articles. J. Softw. Maint. Evol. 19(5), 281–296 (2007)
9. Deerwester, S.C., Dumais, S.T., Landauer, T.K., Furnas, G.W., Harshman, R.A.: Indexing by latent semantic analysis. Journal of the American Society of Information Science 41(6), 391–407 (1990)
10. Dempster, A.P., Laird, N.M., Rubin, D.B.: Maximum likelihood from incomplete data via the EM algorithm. J. Roy. Statist. Soc. Ser. B 39(1), 1–38 (1977)
11. Eick, S.G., Graves, T.L., Karr, A.F., Marron, J.s., Mockus, A.: Does code decay? assessing the evidence from change management data. IEEE Transactions on Software Engineering 27, 1–12 (2001)
12. Enslen, E., Hill, E., Pollock, L.L., Vijay-Shanker, K.: Mining source code to automatically split identifiers for software analysis. In: MSR, pp. 71–80 (2009)
13. Jain, A.K., Murty, M.N., Flynn, P.J.: Data clustering: A review (1999)
14. Kaufman, L., Rousseeuw, P.J.: Finding Groups in Data An Introduction to Cluster Analysis. Wiley Interscience (1990)

15. Koschke, R., Eisenbarth, T.: A framework for experimental evaluation of clustering techniques. In: IWPC, pp. 201–210. IEEE Computer Society (2000)
16. Kuhn, A., Ducasse, S., Gîrba, T.: Semantic clustering: Identifying topics in source code. Information & Software Technology 49(3), 230–243 (2007)
17. Lakhotia, A., Gravley, J.M.: Toward experimental evaluation of subsystem classification recovery techniques. In: Working Conference on Reverse Engineering, pp. 262–269 (1995)
18. Lehman, M.M.: Program evolution. Inf. Process. Manage. 20(1-2), 19–36 (1984)
19. Madani, N., Guerrouj, L., Di Penta, M., Guéhéneuc, Y., Antoniol, G.: Recognizing words from source code identifiers using speech recognition techniques. In: 14th European Conference on Software Maintenance and Reengineering (CSMR 2010), pp. 69–78 (2010)
20. Maletic, J.I., Marcus, A.: Supporting program comprehension using semantic and structural information. In: ICSE, pp. 103–112 (2001)
21. Mancoridis, S., Mitchell, B.S., Rorres, C., Chen, Y., Gansner, E.R.: Using automatic clustering to produce high-level system organizations of source code. In: IWPC 1998: Proceedings of the 6th International Workshop on Program Comprehension, p. 45. IEEE Computer Society, Washington, DC (1998)
22. Manning, C.D., Raghavan, P., Schütze, H.: Introduction to Information Retrieval. Cambridge University Press, New York (2008)
23. Maqbool, O., Babri, H.: Hierarchical clustering for software architecture recovery. IEEE Trans. Softw. Eng. 33(11), 759–780 (2007)
24. McLachlan, G.J., Krishnan, T.: The EM Algorithm and Extensions (Wiley Series in Probability and Statistics), 2nd edn. Wiley Interscience (March 2008)
25. Mclachlan, J., Krishnan, T.: The EM algorithm and Extensions. Wiley interscience (1996)
26. Mitchell, B.S., Mancoridis, S.: On the automatic modularization of software systems using the bunch tool. IEEE Trans. Softw. Eng. 32(3), 193–208 (2006)
27. Murtagh, F.: A survey of recent advances in hierarchical clustering algorithms. The Computer Journal 26(4), 354–359 (1983)
28. Nierstrasz, O., Ducasse, S., Gîrba, T.: The story of moose: an agile reengineering environment. In: ESEC/SIGSOFT FSE, pp. 1–10 (2005)
29. Scanniello, G., D'Amico, A., D'Amico, C., Teodora, D.: Using the kleinberg algorithm and vector space model for software system clustering. In: ICPC 2010: Proceedings of the 18th International Conference on Program Comprehension, IEEE Computer Society, Washington, DC (2010)
30. Scanniello, G., Risi, M., Tortora, G.: Architecture recovery using latent semantic indexing and k-means: an empirical evaluation. In: SEFM 2010: Proceedings of the 2010 IEEE International Conference on Software Engineering and Formal Methods, pp. 103–112. IEEE Computer Society (2010)
31. Tzerpos, V., Holt, R.C.: Mojo: A distance metric for software clusterings. In: WCRE, pp. 187–193 (1999)
32. Tzerpos, V., Holt, R.C.: On the stability of software clustering algorithms. In: IWPC 2000: Proceedings of the 8th International Workshop on Program Comprehension, p. 211. IEEE Computer Society, Washington, DC (2000)
33. van Deursen, A., Hofmeister, C., Koschke, R., Moonen, L., Riva, C.: Symphony: View-driven software architecture reconstruction. In: WICSA, pp. 122–134 (2004)
34. Wen, Z., Tzerpos, V.: An optimal algorithm for mojo distance. In: IWPC 2003: Proceedings of the 11th IEEE International Workshop on Program Comprehension, p. 227. IEEE Computer Society, Washington, DC (2003)

35. Wen, Z., Tzerpos, V.: An effectiveness measure for software clustering algorithms. In: IWPC, pp. 194–203. IEEE Computer Society (2004)
36. Wiggerts, T.A.: Using clustering algorithms in legacy systems remodularization. In: WCRE 1997: Proceedings of the Fourth Working Conference on Reverse Engineering, p. 33. IEEE Computer Society, Washington, DC (1997)
37. Wu, J., Hassan, A.E., Holt, R.C.: Comparison of clustering algorithms in the context of software evolution. In: ICSM 2005: Proceedings of the 21st IEEE International Conference on Software Maintenance, pp. 525–535. IEEE Computer Society, Washington, DC (2005)

Reusing System States by Active Learning Algorithms*

Oliver Bauer, Johannes Neubauer, Bernhard Steffen, and Falk Howar

Technical University Dortmund,
Chair for Programming Systems,
Dortmund, D-44227, Germany
{oliver.bauer,johannes.neubauer,
steffen,falk.howar}@cs.tu-dortmund.de

Abstract. In this paper we present a practical optimization to active automata learning that reduces the average execution time per query as well as the number of actual tests to be executed. Key to our optimization are two observations: (1) establishing well-defined initial conditions for a test (reset) is a very expensive operation on real systems, as it usually involves modifications to the persisted state of the system (e.g., a database). (2) In active learning many of the (sequentially) produced queries are extensions of previous queries. We exploit these observations by using the same test run on a real system for multiple "compatible" queries. We maintain a pool of runs on the real system (system states), and execute only suffixes of queries on the real system whenever possible. The optimizations allow us to apply active learning to an industry-scale web-application running on an enterprise platform: the *Online Conference Service* (*OCS*) an online service-oriented manuscript submission and review system.

1   Introduction

The evolution of the internet – in particular trends like web 2.0 and cloud computing – moves the research focus from systematic and well founded system design to methods for orchestrating and controlling loosely coupled heterogeneous systems including (third party) components that lack proper specification. As an example, the CONNECT Integrated Project [15, 10] aims at overcoming the interoperability barrier between independently provided systems and services by synthesizing required connectors on the fly. In this context, active automata learning [3] is applied in order to complement and complete available knowledge about the involved peers, typically given in terms of (semantically annotated) interface descriptions by means of test-based experimentation. Dependability issues at the system level are mainly addressed in CONNECT at the model-level by means of verification, which abstracts from all the pitfalls that may arise when deploying a system on a realistic enterprise environment facilitating features of application servers like:

---

* This work is supported by the European FP 7 project CONNECT (IST 231167).

A. Moschitti and R. Scandariato (Eds.): EternalS 2011, CCIS 255, pp. 61–78, 2012.
© Springer-Verlag Berlin Heidelberg 2012

- concurrency via threads,
- synchronization and event-handling via messages,
- persistence of the state and business objects.

Learning the emergent overall user-level behavior on an enterprise platform drastically changes the rules of the game: The problem here is not so much the size of the arising models. Focusing on the user level at an adequate level of abstraction keeps the arising models in manageable size. Rather, due to the very complex system landscape, the required test-based experimentation becomes extremely expensive: individual test case may run for many seconds if not minutes, and the system resets for establishing the required independence of individual test cases causes a major problem. Keeping in mind that even learning a very small model with only 30 states easily requires 10,000 tests, and that this number grows quadratically, even in very 'friendly' cases, it is clear that special techniques are required that exploit the characteristics of the chosen setting.

In this paper we propose a new method based on maintaining the states of the overall 'enterprise' system resulting from the tests, with the effect that system resets can be avoided, whenever a new test case is a continuation of a previous test. This optimization is very powerful, in particular when combined with domain-specific knowledge in terms of actions that do not have any effect on the observable behavior (e.g., read-only actions). In our real-life case study on the basis of Springer's Online Conference System *OCS* (see Section 2), which we will discuss in the following in more detail, we observed significant savings:

- without any prerequisite, maintaining the system states saved significantly many resets and executions of many expensive actions,
- additionally taking domain-specific knowledge into account, these savings have been typically tripled.

The reason for this strong impact is the fact that the *OCS*, like many similar services, has a number of actions that do not change state:

- actions that are known to have no observable effect in any state, like a typical read-only action, and
- actions that fail in a certain state, so that the further behavior of the system does not change due to the *OCS*-inherent roll back mechanism.

All this will be explained in detail in Section 5 and illustrated in Section 6.

Related Work: The optimization of active automata learning has been subject to extensive studies. Different learning algorithms for various kinds of automata have been developed, like for Mealy Machines [12, 22, 13, 24], I/O automata [2], Petri nets [7] or Timed automata [9].

Diverse optimizations have been suggested by researchers from the field of active learning theory, most of them for the DFA case from the seminal paper of Angluin [3]. Improvements reach from the algorithmic approach from different data structures like discrimination trees [16] or usage of several local observation tables [4] to a better handling of evidences (counterexamples) that describe how the algorithm refines its hypothesises, c.f. [17, 23] or [14] for an overview of some techniques.

Finding evidence that the algorithm needs to refine its hypothesis is in general undecidable for black-box-systems, however, if the number of states from the unknown system is known, the W-method [5] or Wp-method [8] may be applied. A recent approach for finding such evidences is taken by the ZULU challenge, c.f [11, 6].

Since the number of queries during learning may easily exceed tenth of thousands, different optimizations for usage of domain-specific knowledge have been developed to answer queries that consists of, e.g., symmetric actions. Filters may reduce the number of needed queries by several orders of magnitude [12, 19].

Realizing reset of the System Under Test (SUT) by means of abstraction has been introduced in [26, 1]. To our knowledge, there have been no former attempts to reuse system states in order to save resets.

Outline: The rest of the paper is organized as follows. Section 2 presents a web-based system supporting manuscript submission and review processes as it is facilitated for the case study in Section 6. In Section 3 we provide some theoretical background on query learning and describe briefly the setup to extrapolate Mealy machine models from black-box systems in practice. Section 4 presents the technical basis for our optimization, i.e., reusing system states in detail, while in Section 5 we discuss that domain-specific knowledge can be exploited to further optimize reuse of system states. Section 6 reviews the results of evaluating our optimization in a series of experiments on the OCS. Finally, Section 7 provides a conclusion and plans for our further research on this topic.

2   Online Conference Service

The OCS is an online manuscript submission and review service. It is part of a product line for the Springer Verlag that started in 1999 and evolved over time to include also journal and volume production preparation services. The OCS acts as a decision support system facilitating the process of approving and refusing submissions. Hence, the service follows a well-defined workflow, that is customized for different applications like conferences or journals. Its aim is to assist the efficient cooperation of the different participants in this collaborative process.

In 2009 the OCS underwent a complete redesign and re-implementation, in order to have a more flexible and adaptable system being better suited to verification at the same time. Figure 1 shows a screenshot of the current user interface. It uses industry standard technology and runs on an application server. The new version of the OCS is already in use for real conferences and has proven that it models the work-flow for various conference types effectively. During the preparation of a conference the participants in the decision process have diverse tasks, depending on the progress of the conference schedule. The central purpose of the OCS is the adequate handling of a wealth of independent, but often indirectly

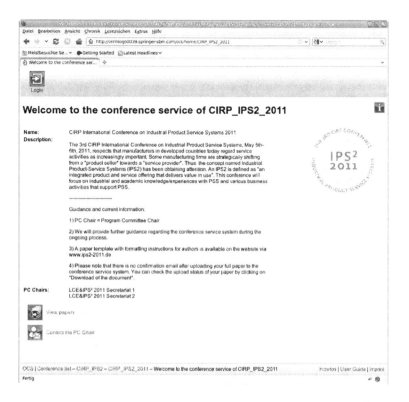

Fig. 1. The start screen of a real conference service for CIRP IPS^2 2011

related, user interactions. From this point of view the OCS is a reactive system with a graphical user interface provided as a web application. Users can decide when they execute their tasks and, in case of multiple tasks, the order in which they process them. They might even reject tasks. Therefore the system has a complex and dynamic user and rights management.

On that note, the OCS is a candidate for a case study for automata learning of reactive systems. Since the OCS has an interface to the business logic offering all functionality being used by the web frontend of the service, we are able to define an abstract alphabet calling the business logic methods via remote method invocation on the real running system. We use a dedicated and isolated installation, without polluting a productive system by learning data and the absence of unintended interference from outside the learning process can be assumed.

As mentioned before, the application to be learned is very complex and as we are conducting actual system invocations instead of resorting to simulation, the amount of tests leads to inacceptable execution time. Furthermore a resulting automaton with hundreds of states is not comprehensible for a human being. The result can be steered with the choice of abstraction in the alphabet. In addition we use filters facilitating domain-specific knowledge in order to have tractable learning procedures.

3 Active Learning

Query learning (or *active learning*) attempts to construct a deterministic finite representation, e.g., a Mealy machine, that matches the behavior of a given target system on the basis of observations of the target system and perhaps some further information on its internal structure. Here, we only summarize the basic aspects of our realization L_M^* for Mealy machines [22], which is based on Angluin's learning algorithm L^* for finite state acceptors [3]. A more elaborate version of this summary and an extended discussion of the practical aspects of active learning is given in [26, 25].

Definition 1. *A Mealy machine is defined as a tuple* $M = \langle Q, q_0, \Sigma, \Gamma, \delta, \gamma \rangle$ *where*

- *Q is a finite nonempty set of* states *(be $n = |Q|$ the size of M),*
- *$q_0 \in Q$ is the* initial state,
- *Σ is a finite* input alphabet,
- *Γ is a finite* output alphabet,
- *$\delta : Q \times \Sigma \to Q$ is the* transition function, *and*
- *$\gamma : Q \times \Sigma \to \Gamma$ is the* output function.

Intuitively, a Mealy machine evolves through states $q \in Q$, and whenever one applies an input symbol (or action) $a \in \Sigma$, the machine moves to a new state according to $\delta(q, a)$.[1]

Query learning is also referred as *active* learning as it constructs automata by actively querying the target system using two kinds of queries. *Membership queries (MQs)* test whether a word (sequence of actions) is in language of the target system (i.e., its set of runs). In practice *MQs* are realized as test runs on a system to be learned. *Equivalence queries (EQs)* compare intermediately constructed hypothesis automata for equivalence with the target system. They will usually be approximated by means of testing, i.e., by *MQs*.

In its basic form, active learning starts with a hypothesis automaton with only one state and refines this automaton on the basis of query results iterating two main steps: *refining the hypothesis* and *testing equivalence* until a state-minimal deterministic (hypothesis) automaton consistent with the target system is produced. Key to achieving this result is the Nerode-like dual characterization of states:

- by a set, $S \subset \Sigma^*$, of *access sequences*. L_M^* will construct such a set S, containing access sequences $s \in \Sigma^*$ to all states of the hypothesis automaton. This characterization of state is too fine, as different words $s_1, s_2 \in S$ may lead to the same state in the target system. Hence L_M^* will maintain a second set, SA, which together with S will cover all transitions of the hypothesis (SA will during the course of learning always be $SA = (S \cdot \Sigma) \setminus S$).

---

[1] To ease presentation, we extend transition- and output function to words in the usual way. For the remainder of the paper, we assume $\delta : Q \times \Sigma^* \to Q$ and $\gamma : Q \times \Sigma^* \to \Gamma$.

– by an ordered set, $D \subset \Sigma^*$, of *distinguishing sequences*. L_M^* realizes the characterization of hypothetical states q simply in terms of vectors $row(s) = \langle r_1, \ldots, r_k \rangle$ (with $r_i \in \Gamma$ and $s \in S \cup SA$), characterizing states by means of subsequent outputs: For $row(s)$, let $r_i = \gamma(\delta(q_0, s), d_i)$ with $d_i \in D$.

L_M^* maintains its observations in an *observation table* (OT) that consists of these sets. The sets, of course, are constructed by means of MQs. The set S will be initialized as $\{\lambda\}$, containing only the access sequence to the initial state; SA will accordingly be initialized as Σ, covering all transitions originating in the initial state. The ordered set D will be initialized as Σ, allowing to identify a state by the output that is produced along the transitions starting in this state.

The learning procedure then continues by refining the hypothesis. This step iterates two phases. The first phase checks whether the constructed automaton is closed under the one-step transitions, i.e., each transition from each state of the hypothesis automaton ends in a well defined state of this very automaton. This is the case if for every $t \in SA$ there exists a $s \in S$ with $row(s) = row(t)$. Otherwise, S will be extended by the corresponding t until *closedness* is established (and SA will be extended accordingly). This extension is guaranteed to result in a unique fixpoint, independent of the order in which the rows are processed.

The second phase then checks whether two access sequences $s_1, s_2 \in S$ with the same bit vector, $row(s_1) = row(s_2)$, have also the same outgoing transitions, a necessary precondition for them to represent the same state. Formally, an OT holding this condition is called *consistent* and needs to satisfy:

$$row(s_1) = row(s_2) \Rightarrow row(s_1 a) = row(s_2 a)$$

for all $s_1, s_2 \in S$ and $a \in \Sigma$. Inconsistencies can be removed by elaborating the set D: the distinguishing future that separates the two target states on the distinguishing transition has simply to be prefixed by the label of this very transition.

Successive iteration of these two phases until closedness and consistency hold is guaranteed to result in an OT from which a unique, well-defined, closed, and complete hypothesis automaton can be derived, whose states are characterized by the bit vectors.

– Every state $q \in Q$ of the hypothesis automaton is reachable by at least one word $s \in S$, i.e., $row(s)$ corresponds to q,
– There exists a transition $\delta(q, a) = q'$ *iff* there exists $s \in S$ with s reaching q (or with $row(s)$ corresponding to q) and $row(s \cdot a)$ corresponding to q',
– The output function can be constructed from the $row()$-vectors as well. As D is initialized as Σ, the values for all $\lambda(q, a)$, where $a \in \Sigma$, are contained in the $row(s)$ vector corresponding to q.

Using an EQ, the learning algorithm tests whether this hypothesis is equivalent to the unknown target system. As soon as an EQ signals success, learning terminates successfully. Otherwise, the EQ will return a counterexample, i.e., a word which distinguishes the hypothesis from the target automaton. All prefixes of a counterexample will be added to S (SA will be extended accordingly). This will lead to inconsistency, which in turn will lead to a new distinguishing suffix [18].

Algorithm 1 summarizes the described procedure of L_M^* in pseudo code. Lines 1-5 depict the initialization-phase, lines 10-13 close the OT, lines 16-18 ensure consistency and through lines 23-27 the default handling of counterexamples is pictured.

The time complexity of learning algorithms is usually measured in terms of consumed MQs and EQs. In practice, however, even the execution of a single action may be time-consuming, since actions can trigger expensive operations on a SUT, e.g., database reads and writes. We will thus always consider both, the number of MQs and the accumulated number of actions executed on a SUT.

Algorithm 1. Learner L_M^*

1: $S \leftarrow \lambda$
2: $SA \leftarrow \Sigma$
3: $D \leftarrow \Sigma$
4: **for** $u \in S \cup SA, e \in D$ **do**
5:     $OT[u, e] \leftarrow MQ(ue)$
6: **repeat**
7:     **while** OT not closed or not consistent **do**
8:         // check for closure
9:         **if** $\exists\, t \in SA : \forall s \in S : row(t) \neq row(s)$ **then**
10:             $S \leftarrow S \cup \{t\}$
11:             $SA \leftarrow (SA \backslash \{t\}) \cup \{ta \mid a \in \Sigma\}$
12:             **for** $e \in D, a \in \Sigma$ **do**
13:                 $OT[ta, e] \leftarrow MQ(tae)$
14:         // check for consistency
15:         **if** $\exists s_1, s_2 \in S, a \in \Sigma : row(s_1) = row(s_2) \wedge row(s_1 a) \neq row(s_2 a)$ **then**
16:             $D \leftarrow D \cup \{ae\}$ // $e \in D$ s.t. $OT[s_1 a, e] \neq OT[s_2 a, e]$
17:             **for** $u \in S \cup SA$ **do**
18:                 $OT[u, ae] \leftarrow MQ(uae)$
19:     $\mathcal{A}_{Hyp} \leftarrow constructHypothesis(S, SA, D)$
20:     $ce \leftarrow EQ(\mathcal{A}_{Hyp})$
21:     // check for conformance
22:     **if** $ce \neq \top$ **then**
23:         $P \leftarrow \{s \mid s \in prefix(ce) \wedge s \notin S\}$
24:         $S \leftarrow S \cup P$
25:         $SA \leftarrow (SA \backslash S) \cup \{ta \mid t \in P, a \in \Sigma, ta \notin S\}$
26:         **for** $u \in (P \cup P\Sigma \backslash S), e \in D$ **do**
27:             $OT[u, e] \leftarrow MQ(ue)$
28: **until** $ce = \top$
29: **return** $\mathcal{A}_{Hyp}$

In the remainder of the paper we will use a small running example to illustrate the presented ideas. The example is a small model of the *OCS*, restricted to submitting a paper to a conference (SP) and further uploading a document (UD) or download a document (DD) from a paper if one exists.

Example 1. Consider the model and the corresponding *OT*, which are shown in Figure 2. In this model, the user is allowed to submit a paper exactly once, while uploads and downloads are unlimited. In addition the user may delete his paper (DP) and start over with a new paper. The output alphabet $\Gamma = \{\checkmark, ↯\}$ indicates successful and unsuccessful actions. The execution of an action may be unsuccessful as it is not allowed by the system or simply because it fails, e.g., a document upload is not possible before a corresponding paper has been submitted. We omit the output in the Mealy automaton for better readability. All edges shown are labeled with 'success' implicitly and the (reflexive) unsuccessful edges are not shown. The *OT* contains 52 entries. The accumulated length of all *MQs* is 148 actions.

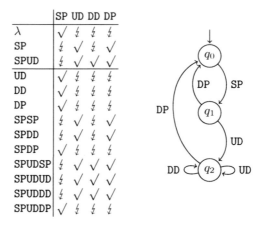

	SP	UD	DD	DP
λ	√	↯	↯	↯
SP	↯	√	↯	√
SPUD	↯	√	√	√
UD	√	↯	↯	↯
DD	√	↯	↯	↯
DP	√	↯	↯	↯
SPSP	↯	√	↯	√
SPDD	↯	√	↯	√
SPDP	√	↯	↯	↯
SPUDSP	↯	√	√	√
SPUDUD	↯	√	√	√
SPUDDD	↯	√	√	√
SPUDDP	√	↯	↯	↯

Fig. 2. Simple Mealy Automaton

4   Reusing System States

In this section we will present our main technical contribution, the reuse algorithm, that allows using the same actual test run for a number of *MQs*. One important prerequisite of active learning is the *independent* execution of *MQs*, i.e., the execution of all tests under identical initial conditions. As discussed in [26], the 'same' initial system state can be provided by different means like executing homing sequences [23], creating new instances of the *SUT* or its whole environment (e.g., a virtual machine), or resetting the persistent storage of the *SUT*.

The latter approaches could be characterized by the notion of *snapshot*. All these procedures have in common, that they are expensive. Using abstraction can be a less expensive alternative providing observational independence between queries (cf. observational equivalent states in [26]). For the *OCS*, e.g., every test can be executed in a unique conference. This way, instead of reinitializing the whole *OCS*, it suffices to create a new conference.

For the remainder of the paper we will assume systems that allow resets to provide independent initial conditions for queries. We will provide an algorithm for such systems that is able to reuse system states on the *SUT* and save execution time by means of the reduction of:

- resets due to the novel approach of reusing system states,
- actions by memorizing the output of already executed queries,
- test runs by exploiting domain-specific knowledge to be executed on the *SUT*.

In the course of learning, as exploration proceeds, the length of access sequences will grow, so a newly *MQ* is likely to contain a prefix for that the output is already known and that was executed on a unique system state. If the abstraction allows us to execute the remaining suffix on this system state we are able to save the otherwise required reset and also the execution of the already executed prefix on this state.

A system state $s \in S$ is a mapping from abstract names to unique identifiers of business objects in the real system. This way s can refer to specific conference, paper, user and document objects, and access them trough their abstract names, so that they are interchangeable. Since the OCS uses a relational database for persistent storage, the primary keys of the business entities are used as unique identifiers. In this paper we write 'conf' for the abstract name for the mapping of the conference object and 'c_1', 'c_2', ... for the unique identifiers. An analogous denotation is used for paper, user and document objects.

We maintain a tree-like data structure $\mathcal{T}$ which we will call the *reuse tree* (see Figure 5). It keeps track of all existing system states in the corresponding *state pool* S. The reuse tree consists of edges that are directed top down and labeled with input behavior regarding input actions $a \in \Sigma$. We omit the output for sake of simplicity. The 'missing' information can be found in the *OT* in Figure 5. Nodes $n_w \in \mathcal{T}$ can contain at most one $s_w \in S$, where $w \in \Sigma^*$ is a path from the root node containing the corresponding input in the respective order. We will denote such nodes with symbol ♦ and, if no system state is available, we will denote it by ◊. Our data structure allows simple operations like inserting a path, adding and removing system states at nodes or getting an output word for a given input word already inserted in the tree.

The reuse algorithm is combined with the learning algorithm as shown in Figure 3. The learner uses the reuse algorithm as a membership oracle: it poses an *MQ* $w \in \Sigma^*$ to the reuse algorithm, which searches for a reference to an already executed prefix $\rho \in \Sigma^*$ of w in its pool of states S that could be reused.

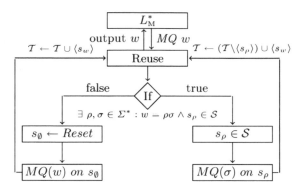

Fig. 3. Workflow of the reuse algorithm

In case such a prefix has been found, it is sufficient to execute the remaining suffix $\sigma \in \Sigma^*$ on the system state corresponding s_ρ and observe the output $o_\sigma \in \Gamma^*$ on the *SUT*. Afterwards, s_ρ can be regarded as $s_{\rho\sigma}$, i.e., s_w. The state will be moved from the node n_ρ to n_w. We call this procedure *state forwarding*. The output from executing σ will be returned to L_M^* as an observed behavior for w.

If no such prefix exists, the reuse algorithm will first perform a reset, e.g., by setting up a new conference as mentioned before. Then, it will execute the *MQ* and store a reference to the system state s_w in its state pool $\mathcal{S}$, before returning the output to L_M^*.

Algorithm 2 illustrates this idea as pseudo code. Since in the course of learning redundant queries may be created, the algorithm contains a simple caching facility (depicted in lines 2 and 3). Suppose $\mathcal{T}$ is able to find some prefix ρ such that s_ρ contains the mapping of abstract identifiers to the corresponding business objects on the target system. If such a s_ρ exists, we could reuse this state by executing the remaining suffix σ updating the data structure, otherwise we have to provide an initial system state by means of a reset.

Table 1. Excerpt from the *OT* of Example 1

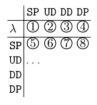

	SP	UD	DD	DP
λ	①	②	③	④
SP	⑤	⑥	⑦	⑧
UD	...			
DD				
DP				

Algorithm 2. Reuse Algorithm

Require: $w \in \Sigma^*$, data structure $\mathcal{T}$
Ensure: $output \in \Gamma^*$
1: // *Check for cached queries*
2: **if** $\mathcal{T}$ *contains* w **then**
3:    **return** *get output for* w *from* $\mathcal{T}$
4: // *Check for reusable system state*
5: $s_\rho \leftarrow$ *get reuseable system state for some* ρ *with* $w = \rho\sigma$ *from* $\mathcal{T}$
6: **if** $s_\rho \neq \perp$ **then**
7:    $s_{\rho\sigma} \leftarrow MQ(\sigma)$ *on* s_ρ
8:    $\mathcal{T} \leftarrow (\mathcal{T} \cup \langle s_{\rho\sigma} \rangle) \setminus \langle s_\rho \rangle$
9:    **return** *output from* $s_{\rho\sigma}$
10: // *Perform normal reset*
11: $s_\emptyset \leftarrow$ *Reset*
12: $s_w \leftarrow MQ(w)$ *on* $s_\emptyset$
13: $\mathcal{T} \leftarrow \mathcal{T} \cup \langle s_w \rangle$
14: **return** *output from* s_w

Example 2. We will demonstrate the presented reuse algorithm for the model from Example 1. We describe how the reuse tree evolves for our running example on the first six MQs from the initialization-phase of L^*_M. The first four MQs need a reset since no prefix exists for which we can reuse an instance (Figure 4). The fifth MQ $w =$ SP SP, can reuse the system state from the first query SP. To answer the query we execute the suffix SP on state s_{SP} only and save the first reset. State s_{SP} will be updated to s_{SPSP} and forwarded from n_{SP} to n_{SPSP}. The sixth MQ $w =$ SP UD again needs a reset, since s_{SP} has been forwarded.

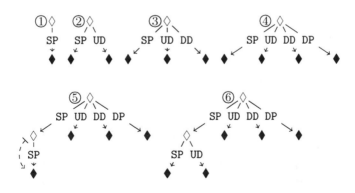

Fig. 4. Reuse trees for the first six queries for Example 1

Figure 6 exemplifies how we save the first reset. For the first query SP we create a new conference c_1 and a new submitter u_1. The action itself submits (successfully) a paper p_1 to the available conference. The system state $s_1 \in \mathcal{S}$ consists of three keys to the available instances. The system state corresponding to the execution of the second MQ UD, which fails, because there is no paper to upload to. So it will result in only two keys for the created conference c_2 and user u_2. Finally the fifth query SP SP reuses the available system state s_1 with its identifier c_1, u_1 and p_1 and querying the remaining suffix will result in a failure output $\notin \Gamma$ since only one paper submission per conference is allowed in our example.

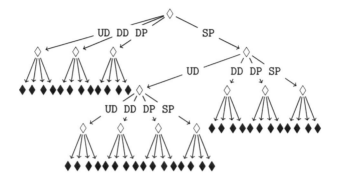

Fig. 5. Final reuse tree for Example 1

Figure 5 illustrates the final reuse tree for Example 1. An instance of a system state is used at most once. Hence, all system states are situated in the leaves of the tree. This result leads to a saving of 12 of originally 52 resets. In addition we saved 24 of 148 actions to be executed on the SUT, i.e. besides saving resets we also accomplish a significant reduction of actions.

5   Domain-Specific Reuse of System States

The reuse algorithm introduced in the previous section is a generic optimization to active learning. In this section we will discuss how domain-specific knowledge can be exploited to further improve reusage of system states. For most systems to be learned, important global properties of the system, or at least of single actions are known prior to learning. The OCS, e.g., is a transaction secure system. If an action fails at some point, the system state will be rolled back. Executing the action will have no persistent effect on the system's state. On the other hand, it could be known that certain actions never influence the behavior of the system on the given level of abstraction. In the case of the OCS, e.g., downloading papers is known to be such an action. Information of this kind can be exploited to optimize the reuse tree.

Let us properly define *failure invariance*. We partition the output alphabet in success and failure outputs $\Gamma = \Gamma_s \cup \Gamma_f$ with $\Gamma_s \cap \Gamma_f = \emptyset$.

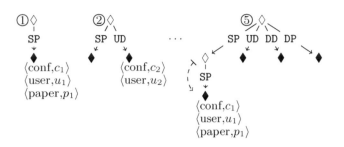

Fig. 6. Evolution of system states $\mathcal{S}$ in Example 1

Definition 2. *We call a SUT* failure invariant, *iff*

$$\forall a \in \Sigma : \ \forall q \in Q : \ \gamma(q,a) \in \Gamma_f \ \Rightarrow \ \delta(q,a) = q.$$

Intuitively, a *SUT* is failure invariant if all transitions with failure outputs are reflexive, i.e., do not change the system's state.

We further define a set $\Sigma_i \subseteq \Sigma$ of actions, for which the observable system behavior is invariant.

Definition 3. *We call a SUT* action invariant *for an action a iff*

$$\forall q \in Q : \ \delta(q,a) = q.$$

Key to exploiting these properties in the reuse algorithm is the idea that in the case of an observed failure output or after executing an action invariant action it is not necessary to move the system state downwards in the reuse tree. We relax the tree properties of our data structure to allow reflexive edges. Instead of forwarding a state in the tree after executing an action a that resulted in a failure or that is from Σ_i, the state now remains in its node and is reusable for the next query sharing the same prefix. This is indicated by adding a reflexive edge if the output symbol is contained within Γ_f

This optimization may sometimes even allow answering not yet posed *MQs* without even executing any action on the *SUT*. Suppose $a \in \Sigma_i$, and a word $w = abcac \in \Sigma^*$ with s_w. Then s_w could be reused not only for ww', $w' \in \Sigma^*$, but also, e.g., for bcc or $bcaac$. We denote a query that can be answered by the tree due to such an unfolding of reflexive edges as a *pumped query*.

Example 3. Figure 7 illustrates how the tree evolves for the first eight queries if we use domain-specific knowledge on failure outputs. The remaining twelve queries from the initialization phase of the *OT* (c.f. Table 1) will be answered directly because an output can be extruded from the tree facilitating a pumped query.

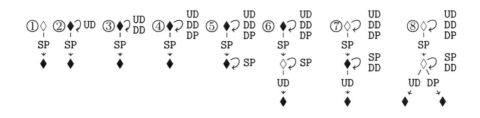

Fig. 7. Pumped queries in Example 1

Figure 8 depicts the final reuse tree corresponding to Example 1 if we exploit outputs that indicate failure. Note that in Figure 8 not only the leaves contain system states. We achieve a reduction from 52 resets down to 10. Only 50 of 148 actions need to be executed on the *SUT*.

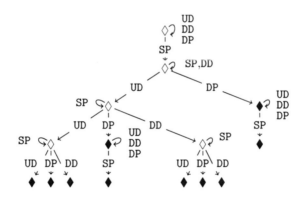

Fig. 8. Reusage with failure exploitation

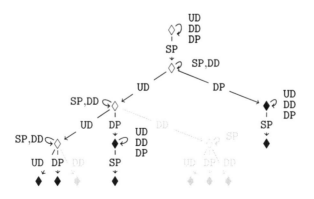

Fig. 9. Reusage with failure and action invariance

Figure 9 pictures the effect of using domain-specific knowledge on both action and failure invariance. It shows the effect of using the knowledge, that the system is invariant under the download action DD. Compared to Figure 8 two branches (shaded in light gray) have been collapsed and are now represented through reflexive edges. Both branches represent the reflexive edge $\delta(q_2, \text{DD}) = q_2$ in Example 1. Exploiting the latter property further reduces the necessary resets from 10 to 6 and the executed actions from 50 to 35.

6   Case Study

The reuse algorithm is implemented as an addition to the NGLL [20], an automata learning framework[2]. For our case study the real world application OCS serves as SUT[3] (please refer to [21]).

Hence, MQs are realized via test runs on the OCS, utilizing method calls on the business interface as input actions. In order to provide identical conditions for all tests, the reset is achieved by means of abstraction: every test is executed using a new conference and a new user (invisible to the learning algorithm). The *system state* s maps abstract identifiers like 'conference' and 'user' to unique database identifiers. Submitting a paper additionally adds a mapping from 'paper' to the unique identifier of the corresponding paper in the SUT.

We learned various models with a growing number of actions. Starting with a test case nearly the same as described in Example 1 (only without the DP action), we added more actions successively, e.g., for interrupting phases, reviewer assignment, report submission or accepting or refusing submissions. We chose six different setups, using L_{M}^{*} in conjunction with the reuse algorithm for extrapolating behavioral models from the OCS. Each experiment was performed on a dedicated instance of the running application server with an initially empty database.

Table 2 states statistics on the effect of reusing system states with different settings. The table is organized into columns for the number of states in the final model $|Q|$, the number of actions $|\Sigma|$ and the number of required MQs. The MQs are subdivided into resets, reuses and pumped queries. The remaining three columns depict the average time for a reset, the estimated running time for resets without reusing system states and the observed runtime of the whole experiment (note that this also includes the execution of actions corresponding to the execution of the MQs).

For case (a) we learned Example 1 (the DP action was not included) without EQs and with direct reusage only. Since we did not exploit domain-specific knowledge in this experiment we get no pumped queries. In case (b) we used the

---

[2] NGLL is available at **http://www.learnlib.de**

[3] The test runs have been executed on a Sun Fire X2200 with two dual core AMD Opteron 2214 CPUs clocked at 2.2GHz and 8GB DDR2/667 ECC memory. Ubuntu 10.04 served as the operating system. The OCS has been deployed on a JBoss-5.1.0.GA with the Java Runtime Environment SUN JVM 1.6.0_18 for 64-bit systems.

Table 2. Statistics on some extrapolated models

			membership queries					
$|Q|$	$|\Sigma|$	MQs	Resets	Reuses	Pumped	Avg. reset	Est. reset	Observed runtime
(a) 3	3	30	21	9	0	1.8s.	56s.	40s.
(b) 11	5	280	31	84	165	2.3s.	10m	1m 25s.
(c) 11	5	280	17	78	185	2.1s.	9m	48s.
(d) 40	9	3882	137	757	2988	3.2s.	3h 27m	10m 30s
(e) 66	13	12210	646	2514	9050	4.1s.	13h 52m	53m 50s
(f) 160	18	56284	5598	12168	38518	12.7s.	over 8 days	$\approx$ 22h

same actions as before and added two additional actions. We exploited knowledge about failure invariance only. Nearly 90 percent of resets have been saved, whereas the most significant savings have been done by pumping queries. To show the impact of invariant actions we marked the download action correspondingly in case (c). The resets have been reduced further. Although the reuses have been reduced the runtime of the experiment decreases. For case (d) we have enhanced the alphabet where we refined the first hypothesis by a hand tailored counterexample (to consider necessary MQs only). The second EQ was skipped in this case. As we can see, about 96.5% resets have been saved. Since the database and the system load has grown to previous experiments the average reset time also has been increased. In case (e) an automaton with even more states has been learned in less than one hour. About 94.7% of resets have been saved. The time reduction on the experiment already shows the impact of this savings. In the last case we learned a almost complete workflow in the OCS, considering different phases, e.g., the submission-, review- and final-phase, as well as the different participating roles, e.g., pc chairs, pc members or reviewers. Using five additional actions to case (e) results in an increased amount of queries for case (f). As in case (e) we provided the same hand tailored counterexample.

As the statistics show, reusing system states drastically reduces the overall running time of learning realistic systems like the OCS. Infering system behavior is a time consuming task and reusing system states can help archieving this extrapolation in a reasonable time.

7   Conclusions

In this paper we have presented an optimization to active learning that is able to reuse existing system states for several membership queries and saves the execution of resets on the SUT. Our implementation results in considerable savings on execution time on real systems, where resets tend to be expensive operations. We have discussed, how domain-specific knowledge can be applied to further improve reusage of prefixes of MQs, i.e actions. This comprises failure and action invariances of a system as well as an advanced cache facility enabling to omit complete test runs by pumping posed queries. We have evaluated our approach in a series of experiments on a real-word enterprise application, the *Online Conference Service*.

We are planning to work on heuristics that improve reusage of system states even further. The reuse algorithm could then 'learn', e.g., action invariances of the system.

References

[1] Aarts, F., Blom, J., Bohlin, T., Chen, Y.-F., Howar, F., Jonsson, B., Merten, M., Nagel, R., Sabetta, A., Soleimanifard, S., Steffen, B., Uijen, J., Wilk, T., Windmuller, S.: Establishing basis for learning algorithms (2010)

[2] Aarts, F., Vaandrager, F.: Learning I/O Automata. In: Gastin, P., Laroussinie, F. (eds.) CONCUR 2010. LNCS, vol. 6269, pp. 71–85. Springer, Heidelberg (2010)

[3] Angluin, D.: Learning Regular Sets from Queries and Counterexamples. Information and Computation 75(2), 87–106 (1987)

[4] Balcázar, J.L., Díaz, J., Gavaldà, R.: Algorithms for Learning Finite Automata from Queries: A Unified View. In: Advances in Algorithms, Languages, and Complexity, pp. 53–72 (1997)

[5] Chow, T.S.: Testing Software Design Modeled by Finite-State Machines. IEEE Trans. on Software Engineering 4(3), 178–187 (1978)

[6] Combe, D., de la Higuera, C., Janodet, J.-C.: Zulu: An Interactive Learning Competition. In: Yli-Jyrä, A., Kornai, A., Sakarovitch, J., Watson, B. (eds.) FSMNLP 2009. LNCS, vol. 6062, pp. 139–146. Springer, Heidelberg (2010)

[7] Esparza, J., Leucker, M., Schlund, M.: Learning Workflow Petri Nets. In: Lilius, J., Penczek, W. (eds.) PETRI NETS 2010. LNCS, vol. 6128, pp. 206–225. Springer, Heidelberg (2010)

[8] Fujiwara, S., von Bochmann, G., Khendek, F., Amalou, M., Ghedamsi, A.: Test Selection Based on Finite State Models. IEEE Trans. on Software Engineering 17(6), 591–603 (1991)

[9] Grinchtein, O., Jonsson, B., Pettersson, P.: Inference of Event-Recording Automata Using Timed Decision Trees. In: Baier, C., Hermanns, H. (eds.) CONCUR 2006. LNCS, vol. 4137, pp. 435–449. Springer, Heidelberg (2006)

[10] Howar, F., Jonsson, B., Merten, M., Steffen, B., Cassel, S.: On Handling Data in Automata Learning - Considerations from the CONNECT Perspective. In: Margaria, T., Steffen, B. (eds.) ISoLA 2010, Part II. LNCS, vol. 6416, pp. 221–235. Springer, Heidelberg (2010)

[11] Howar, F., Steffen, B., Merten, M.: From ZULU to RERS - Lessons Learned in the ZULU Challenge. In: Margaria, T., Steffen, B. (eds.) ISoLA 2010, Part I. LNCS, vol. 6415, pp. 687–704. Springer, Heidelberg (2010)

[12] Hungar, H., Niese, O., Steffen, B.: Domain-Specific Optimization in Automata Learning. In: Hunt Jr., W.A., Somenzi, F. (eds.) CAV 2003. LNCS, vol. 2725, pp. 315–327. Springer, Heidelberg (2003)

[13] Hungar, H., Steffen, B.: Behavior-based model construction. Int. J. Softw. Tools Technol. Transf. 6(1), 4–14 (2004)

[14] Irfan, M.N., Oriat, C., Groz, R.: Angluin style finite state machine inference with non-optimal counterexamples. In: Proceedings of the First International Workshop on Model Inference In Testing (2010)

[15] Issarny, V., Steffen, B., Jonsson, B., Blair, G.S., Grace, P., Kwiatkowska, M.Z., Calinescu, R., Inverardi, P., Tivoli, M., Bertolino, A., Sabetta, A.: CONNECT Challenges: Towards Emergent Connectors for Eternal Networked Systems. In: ICECCS, pp. 154–161 (2009)

[16] Kearns, M.J., Vazirani, U.V.: An Introduction to Computational Learning Theory. MIT Press, Cambridge (1994)

[17] Maler, O., Pnueli, A.: On the Learnability of Infinitary Regular Sets. Information and Computation 118(2), 316–326 (1995)

[18] Margaria, T., Niese, O., Raffelt, H., Steffen, B.: Efficient test-based model generation for legacy reactive systems. In: HLDVT 2004: Proceedings of the High-Level Design Validation and Test Workshop, Ninth IEEE International, pp. 95–100. IEEE Computer Society, Washington, DC (2004)

[19] Margaria, T., Raffelt, H., Steffen, B.: Knowledge-based relevance filtering for efficient system-level test-based model generation. Innovations in Systems and Software Engineering 1(2), 147–156 (2005)

[20] Merten, M., Steffen, B., Howar, F., Margaria, T.: Next Generation Learnlib. In: Abdulla, P.A., Leino, K.R.M. (eds.) TACAS 2011. LNCS, vol. 6605, pp. 220–223. Springer, Heidelberg (2011)

[21] Neubauer, J., Margaria, T., Steffen, B.: The ocs case study. In: FMICS Handbook on Industrial Critical Systems (to appear, 2011)

[22] Niese, O.: An Integrated Approach to Testing Complex Systems. PhD thesis, University of Dortmund, Germany (2003)

[23] Rivest, R.L., Schapire, R.E.: Inference of finite automata using homing sequences. Inf. Comput. 103(2), 299–347 (1993)

[24] Shahbaz, M., Groz, R.: Inferring Mealy Machines. In: Cavalcanti, A., Dams, D.R. (eds.) FM 2009. LNCS, vol. 5850, pp. 207–222. Springer, Heidelberg (2009)

[25] Steffen, B., Howar, F., Merten, M.: Introduction to Active Automata Learning from a Practical Perspective. In: Bernardo, M., Issarny, V. (eds.) SFM 2011. LNCS, vol. 6659, pp. 256–296. Springer, Heidelberg (2011)

[26] Steffen, B., Howar, F., Merten, M., Margaria, T.: Practical aspects of active automata learning. In: FMICS Handbook on Industrial Critical Systems (to appear, 2011)

Inferring Affordances Using Learning Techniques

Amel Bennaceur[1], Richard Johansson[2], Alessandro Moschitti[2],
Romina Spalazzese[3], Daniel Sykes[1], Rachid Saadi[1], and Valérie Issarny[1]

[1] INRIA, Paris-Rocquencourt, France
[2] University of Trento, Italy
[3] University of L'Aquila, L'Aquila, Italy

Abstract. Interoperability among heterogeneous systems is a key
challenge in today's networked environment, which is characterised by
continual change in aspects such as mobility and availability. Automated
solutions appear then to be the only way to achieve interoperability with
the needed level of flexibility and scalability. While necessary, the techniques used to achieve interaction, working from the highest application
level to the lowest protocol level, come at a substantial computational
cost, especially when checks are performed indiscriminately between systems in unrelated domains. To overcome this, we propose to use machine learning to extract the high-level functionality of a system and
thus restrict the scope of detailed analysis to systems likely to be able to
interoperate.

1 Introduction

We live in a world populated by highly heterogeneous, networked, mobile and
pervasive systems and services. Such heterogeneity may span the application
layer, the middleware layer, and the underlying communication infrastructure.
Interaction between these systems, where feasible, is customarily achieved
through diverse ad hoc means for specific pairs of systems in a particular environment. *Principled* automatic composition can bring a labour-saving benefit–
through generalisation over classes of systems–and can provide the flexibility
needed to cope with rapidly changing contexts, dynamic service availability and
user mobility.

Automatic service composition has three main phases: discovery of what services exist in the current scope; finding pairs or sets of services which are compatible, so as to make composition possible; and the actual process of connecting one
system to another. The second step of finding matching pairs of systems can be a
computationally costly procedure, both in terms of the number of combinations
of systems which have been discovered, but also in terms of the deep behavioural
(or protocol) analyses used to determine if a single pair is compatible.

Hence it is unreasonable to perform matching with all systems every time a
new system is discovered. Indeed, detailed matching between heterogeneous systems working in wildly different application domains is nonsensical: the word pro-
cessor on a traveller's laptop need not be compared against the air-traffic control

A. Moschitti and R. Scandariato (Eds.): EternalS 2011, CCIS 255, pp. 79–87, 2012.
© Springer-Verlag Berlin Heidelberg 2012

infrastructure simply because he is situated inside the airport. On the other hand, matching against a document translation service may in fact be of some use.

What is required is a notion of *category of systems*; things that speak about the same domain. Then matching can be restricted to combinations falling within a given category. For this purpose, we define an *affordance* which represents the high-level functionality (capability) of a given system with reference to an ontology which specifies the domain of interest. A system may have several affordances, representing different facets of its functionality, each of which may even relate to a different domain.

In addition to restricting the scope of matching, affordances can further increase the efficiency of composition by exploiting a structured repository wherein system descriptions are stored according to the matching relation. Structuring the repository in this manner reduces the number of comparisons which need to be made when a new system is discovered, even within a given domain. Figure 1 illustrates the linear speed up of matching when affordances are used.

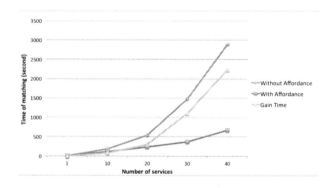

Fig. 1. Time of matching with and without using affordances

These benefits can only be reaped, however, when all systems are annotated with their respective affordances: a substantial effort for the great numbers of legacy systems, which provide only their interface description. However, it is worthwhile considering what process the programmer may go through when assigning an affordance. Given a set of "universally" agreed concepts in the ontology, the programmer can examine the interface and its documentation to determine which concepts best describe the broad category and functionality of the system. It goes without saying that to achieve this, the natural language descriptions and identifiers (such as method names) present in the interface will be used to make the classification.

We propose to use machine learning to automate the extraction of affordances from the interface description by classifying the natural-language text according to a pre-defined ontology of systems. Such an approach can fill the gap when a discovered system does not have a programmer-assigned affordance.

In the following, we set out in more detail the context of our problem, focussing on services, and discuss techniques that may be used to realise the approach.

2   Automatic Service Composition

To compose services automatically we can make use of a theory [5] for the automated synthesis of *mediating connectors* (also called *mediators*) that has been defined elsewhere [1]. That is, the service composition problem can be seen as an instance of the kind of problems the theory is able to model and solve.

More specifically, to compose services we need to: (i) *discover* the available ones, (ii) find *matching* pairs among them, and (iii) *synthesise* mediators that adapt the services behaviours allowing them to interoperate.

Our approach to dynamic service composition and interoperability is illustrated in Figure 2.

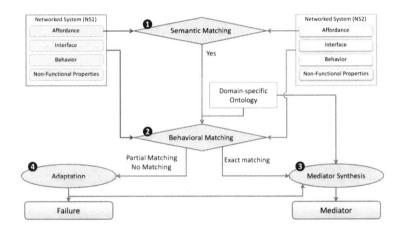

Fig. 2. Approach to dynamic interoperability

Two descriptions of networked systems (NSs) are given, including their interface, behaviour, non-functional properties and affordance descriptions. The first step consists of checking the compatibility of their *affordances*, high-level functionality, through the use of semantic matching (❶). Then, in the successful cases, a behavioural matching (❷) is performed by reasoning about both the NSs descriptions and the ontologies characterising their actions. In the case of exact behavioural matching, a mediator is synthesised (❸) based on the results of the reasoning in the previous step, while in the case of partial matching, a protocol adaptation (❹) is needed before the mediator synthesis. This process highlights the central role of the semantic matching of affordances in reducing the overall computation by acting as a kind of filter for the subsequent behavioural matching.

2.1   Affordances

An *affordance* denotes a high-level functionality provided to or required from the networked environment. Concretely, an affordance is specified as a tuple:

$$Aff = \langle Type, F, I, O \rangle$$

where:

- *Type* stands for a required (noted *Req*), provided (noted *Prov*) or required and provided (noted *Req_Prov*) affordance.
- F gives the semantics of the functionality associated with the affordance in terms of an ontology concept.
- I (resp. O) specifies the set of inputs (resp. outputs) of the affordance, which is defined as a tuple $\langle i_1, ..., i_n \rangle$ (resp. $\langle o_1, ..., o_m \rangle$) with each i_l (resp. o_k) being an ontology concept.

For example, $\langle Prov, AuctionHouse, \langle Goods \rangle, \langle Money \rangle \rangle$ is an affordance describing the provision of *AuctionHouse* functionality with an input of *Goods* and an output of *Money*.

The first step in identifying the possible *compatibility* of two networked systems is to assess whether they respectively provide and require semantically matching affordances. For example, a *Procurement* application, being a kind of *Buyer*, may match the above *AuctionHouse*, as a specific kind of *Seller*. Once a functional match is found at the affordance level, the more costly behavioural and non-functional matching can be performed.

2.2   Legacy Applications

Unfortunately, legacy applications do not normally provide affordance descriptions. We must therefore rely upon an engineer to provide them manually, or find some automated means to extract the probable affordance from the interface description. Note that it is not strictly necessary to have a guaranteed correct affordance since falsely-identified matches will be caught in the subsequent detailed checks.

In this paper we focus on using machine learning to extract affordances from interface descriptions. Moreover we focus on the functional concept F of the affordance, rather than the inputs and outputs, though the overall approach would be notionally unchanged. Learning the inputs and outputs would require a straightforward division of the interface into parts which refer to data and those which refer to the functionality, and performing the learning procedure on each independently.

3   Affordance Learning

This section provides an example interface description to bring the affordance learning problem into focus.

3.1   Typical Interface

Listing 1.1 shows a small fragment of the WSDL interface description of the popular eBay [2] web service.

Listing 1.1. Ebay WSDL interface description

```
<!--  Call :  AddItem  -->
<xs:element  name="AddItemRequest"
              type="ns:AddItemRequestType"/>
<xs:complexType  name="AddItemRequestType">
  <xs:annotation>
    <xs:documentation>
      Defines a single new item and lists it  on a specified eBay site.
       <b>Also for Half.com</b>.
      Returns the item ID for the new listing, and returns fees
      the seller will incur for the listing (not including the Final
      Value Fee, which cannot be calculated until the item is sold).
    </xs:documentation>
    <xs:appinfo>
    <RelatedCalls>
      AddFixedPriceItem, AddItems, AddToItemDescription, GetItem,
      GetItemRecommendations, GetSellerList, RelistItem, ReviseItem,
      VerifyAddItem
    </RelatedCalls>
    <SeeLink>
      <Title>Listing an Item</Title>
      <URL>http://developer.ebay.com/...</URL>
    </SeeLink>
    <SeeLink>
      <Title>Listing Items</Title>
      <URL>http://developer.ebay.com/...</URL>
    </SeeLink>
    ...
```

This example provides extensive English text in both the documentation and the terms used in message and type names. Note that the complete description is approximately 130k lines long. In order to handle less verbose descriptions, documentation acquired from alternative sources such as `http://webservices.seekda.com/` can be used. It would not take an engineer, or indeed a layperson, long to determine the approximate purpose of the service, relying on key words such as 'item', 'seller' and 'fee'. A concept from a pre-determined ontology, such as *AuctionHouse*, could then be assigned. Given such a description we propose to use machine learning to infer the appropriate affordance for the service.

3.2   Learning Problem

The problem we are considering, then, is to find a function f which, given a parsed interface description with only the natural-language terms remaining, determines with some confidence the concept most appropriate for that service:

$$f : Interface \rightarrow (Concept \times Confidence)$$

To achieve this, we provide a number of examples as training data relating interfaces to concepts: *Interface × Concept*. These examples are acquired by searching for web service descriptions in online repositories, e.g., `webservicelist.com` and `xmethods.com`, and manually assigning to each a concept. The learning technique employed should then be able to generalise from the examples to produce an f to classify new examples. It is necessary to have a number of example interfaces for each concept we wish to assign to services.

Note that the problem could be tackled at (at least) two levels of granularity: the concepts could indicate the broad category of service within a "universal" ontology (taxonomy), or they could indicate a more specific service type within an ontology restricted to a specific domain. The learning problem is the same for both; all that changes is the breadth of automation we can achieve versus the depth of the domain. Arbitrarily increasing the breadth and depth of the ontology will impact confidence as it becomes increasingly likely that concepts are ambiguous.

4   Potential Solution: Machine Learning of Categorisers

We believe that the problem of affordance learning can draw many lessons from the long tradition of research in *text categorisation*: the problem of assigning a given document to one or more categories. The complexity of the system of categories may be low in some cases, such as a binary set {POSITIVE, NEGATIVE} when classifying a customer review as positive or negative [12], and higher in other cases, such as the various structured classification systems used in library science. The main tool for implementing modern systems for automatic document classification systems is machine learning based on vector space document representations.

4.1   Introduction to Machine Learning

In general, we define machine learning as the problem of inducing a function (or system of functions) from a given data set. We may discern two main strands of machine learning methods: *supervised* and *unsupervised* methods.

The most archetypical problem setting in machine learning is the supervised setting. In supervised learning, the learning mechanism is provided with a (typically finite) set of labelled examples: a set of pairs $T = \{\langle x, y \rangle\}$. The goal is to make use of the example set T to induce a function f such that generally $f(x) = y$ for future, unseen instances of (x, y) pairs. Supervised learning methods in most cases learn much more accurate classifiers than their unsupervised counterparts, but require a human-annotated training set of significant size: the bigger the better. Examples of supervised learning methods commonly used include Support Vector Machines [3], which have been extensively studied for the problem of text categorisation [6]. For the problem of automatic association of WSDL interface descriptions with concepts, we thus need to gather a large set of interface descriptions and manually assign one or more concepts to every description.

As opposed to the supervised setting, the problem definition in unsupervised learning instead assumes the examples to be unlabelled, i.e. $T = \{x\}$. In order to be able to come up with anything useful when no supervision is provided, the learning mechanism needs a bias that guides the learning process. The most well-known example of unsupervised learning is probably k-means clustering [8], where the learner learns to categorise objects into broad categories even though the categories were not given a priori. More complex examples include grammar induction methods from raw text.

In addition to two main subfields of learning methods there are of course outliers and hybrids, such as *semisupervised* learning: Since it is costly to produce manually labelled training data, in some situations only a small labelled example set $T_s = \{\langle x, y \rangle\}$ is provided, while there is also available a larger unlabelled example set $T_u = \{x\}$. Semisupervised learning methods are able to make use of the labelled data T_s in combination with the unlabelled data T_u in order to improve over a plain supervised learner making use of T_s only. Another interesting learning paradigm is *active learning*, where the learning mechanism is able to select particularly informative unlabelled examples from an unlabelled dataset and ask an oracle (a human annotator or some sort of automatic mechanism) for a labelling. Typically, active learners are able to achieve a more efficient use of the training data than normal supervised learners, since their behaviour is more targeted towards distinguishing the difficult cases.

4.2   Representations for Categorisation

In order to be able to apply standard supervised or unsupervised machine learning methods for building categorisers, we need to represent the objects we want to classify by extracting informative *features*. For categorisation of documents, the standard representation method maps every document into a vector space using the *bag-of-words* approach [13]. In this method, every word in the vocabulary is associated with a dimension of the vector space, allowing the document to be mapped into the vector space simply by computing the occurrence frequencies of each word. The bag-of-words representation is considered the standard representation underlying most document classification approaches, and attempts to incorporate more complex structural information have mostly been unsuccessful for the task of categorisation of single documents [10] although more successful for complex relational classification tasks [9].

However, the task of classifying WSDL interface descriptions is different from classifying raw documents: the interface descriptions are *semi-structured* rather than unstructured, and the representation method clearly needs to take this fact into account, for instance by separating the vector space into regions representing the respective parts of the WSDL description. For instance, the description in Figure 1.1 contains a general documentation part in free text, as well as a number of textual descriptions of the methods defined by the interface.

In addition to the text, we believe that the various semi-structured identifiers should be included in the feature representation, most importantly the names of the methods defined by the interface but also the methods listed in the `RelatedCalls` section. The inclusion of identifiers will be important since 1) the textual content of the identifiers is often highly informative of the functionality provided by the respective methods; 2) the free text documentation is not mandatory and may not always be present. Extracting useful bag-of-words representations from the identifiers will likely have to use splitting heuristics relying on the presence of indicators such as underscores or CamelCase.

5   Conclusions

Principled automatic composition is the only means to overcome the manifold difficulties inherent in the problem of interoperability of diverse, heterogeneous systems. In contrast to incidental *ad hoc* solutions, automatic composition brings such benefits as scalability, self-adaptation, flexibility, resilience to faults, and tolerance of dynamic availability and user mobility. Affordances are the first weapon in attacking the problem, by categorising systems and so avoiding unnecessarily deep checks on systems whose high-level functionality is utterly different.

Affordances need not be especially precise—we are not looking for a surgical strike—since the detailed work is handled by behavioural and other compatibility checks. For this reason we are able to take advantage of machine learning to provide us with affordances when they have not been provided by the programmer. Techniques such as support vector machines can categorise free text according to a pre-defined ontology of systems, however it may be beneficial to treat the WSDL interface description as a semi-structured document, by, for example, separating method, input and output identifiers from pure documentation.

In addition to experimenting with different categorisers and the structure of the input, the provision and the generality of the ontology of systems poses a challenge. While we do not wish to limit the scope of the approach to a particular domain, having overly general concepts will again lead to unnecessary deep compatibility checks.

A number of similar approaches exist, particularly in the field of web services, such as [11,7,4], from which we can draw guidance. However, their aims and context often differ. In our case, the extraction of an affordance to categorise systems promises to bring such benefits as well-targeted compatibility checking, efficient storage of descriptions, and a potential for decentralisation.

Acknowledgments. This work is done as part of the European FP7 ICT FET CONNECT project (http://connect-forever.eu/).

References

1. CONNECT Annex I: Description of Work. FET IP CONNECT EU project, FP7 grant agreement number 231167, http://connect-forever.eu/
2. eBay WSDL, http://developer.ebay.com/webservices/latest/ebaySvc.wsdl
3. Boser, B., Guyon, I., Vapnik, V.: A training algorithm for optimal margin classifiers. In: Proceedings of the Fifth Annual Workshop on Computational Learning Theory (1992)

4. Heß, A., Kushmerick, N.: Learning to Attach Semantic Metadata to Web Services. In: Fensel, D., Sycara, K., Mylopoulos, J. (eds.) ISWC 2003. LNCS, vol. 2870, pp. 258–273. Springer, Heidelberg (2003)
5. Inverardi, P., Issarny, V., Spalazzese, R.: A Theory of Mediators for Eternal Connectors. In: Margaria, T., Steffen, B. (eds.) ISoLA 2010. LNCS, vol. 6416, pp. 236–250. Springer, Heidelberg (2010)
6. Joachims, T.: Learning to Classify Text Using Support Vector Machines. Kluwer Academic Publishers (2002)
7. Klusch, M., Kapahnke, P., Zinnikus, I.: Sawsdl-mx2: A machine-learning approach for integrating semantic web service matchmaking variants. In: ICWS (2009)
8. MacQueen, J.B.: Some methods for classification and analysis of multivariate observations. In: Proceedings of 5th Berkeley Symposium on Mathematical Statistics and Probability (1967)
9. Moschitti, A.: Kernel methods, syntax and semantics for relational text categorization. In: Proc. of CIKM (2008)
10. Moschitti, A., Basili, R.: Complex Linguistic Features for Text Classification: A Comprehensive Study. In: McDonald, S., Tait, J.I. (eds.) ECIR 2004. LNCS, vol. 2997, pp. 181–196. Springer, Heidelberg (2004)
11. Oldham, N., Thomas, C., Sheth, A.P., Verma, K.: Meteor-s Web Service Annotation Framework with Machine Learning Classification. In: Cardoso, J., Sheth, A.P. (eds.) SWSWPC 2004. LNCS, vol. 3387, pp. 137–146. Springer, Heidelberg (2005)
12. Pang, B., Lee, L., Vaithyanathan, S.: Thumbs up? Sentiment classification using machine learning techniques. In: Proceedings of the 2002 Conference on Empirical Methods in Natural Language Processing (2002)
13. Salton, G., Wong, A., Yang, C.S.: A vector space model for automatic indexing. Tech. Rep. TR74-218, Cornell University (1974)

Predicting User Tags Using Semantic Expansion

Krishna Chandramouli, Tomas Piatrik, and Ebroul Izquierdo

Multimedia and Vision Research Group
School of Electronic Engineering and Computer Science
Queen Mary, University of London, Mile End Road, E1 4NS, London
{krishna.chandramouli,tomas.piatrik,ebroul.izquierdo}@eecs.qmul.ac.uk

Abstract. Manually annotating content such as Internet videos, is an intellectually expensive and time consuming process. Furthermore, keywords and community-provided tags lack consistency and present numerous irregularities. Addressing the challenge of simplifying and improving the process of tagging online videos, which is potentially not bounded to any particular domain, we present an algorithm for predicting user-tags from the associated textual metadata in this paper. Our approach is centred around extracting named entities exploiting complementary textual resources such as Wikipedia and Wordnet. More specifically to facilitate the extraction of semantically meaningful tags from a largely unstructured textual corpus we developed a natural language processing framework based on GATE architecture. Extending the functionalities of the in-built GATE named entities, the framework integrates a bag-of-articles algorithm for effectively searching through the Wikipedia articles for extracting relevant articles. The proposed framework has been evaluated against MediaEval 2010 Wild Wild Web dataset, which consists of large collection of Internet videos.

Keywords: tag prediction, video indexing, user-contributed metadata, speech recognition, evaluation.

1 Introduction

With the advances in computer technologies and the advent of World Wide Web (WWW), there has been an explosion in the amount and complexity of digital media that is being generated, stored, transmitted, analysed and accessed. Much of this information is multimedia in nature, which includes digital images, video, audio, graphics and textual data. These so-called "online video repositories" enable the users to creatively share thoughts, ideas not only among social peers, but rather enable them to publish these resources to a much wider audience. As a consequence, every online user has been transformed into the role of a broadcaster. In efforts to be heard, there is an increasing interest in associating these media items with free-text annotations. These free-text annotations commonly range from a simple video title to much more detailed description of the video content. Often these textual descriptions are aimed at summarising the content of the video in addition to contextualising the video content. Indexing these

A. Moschitti and R. Scandariato (Eds.): EternalS 2011, CCIS 255, pp. 88–99, 2012.

large-amount of video datasets has been a challenging research issue which until now has been heavily relied up on "user-tags". The disadvantages of manual textual tagging has been studied over the years and the three main problems associated with it include (i) manual labour; (ii) differences in the interpretation of the media items; (iii) inconsistency of the keyword assignments among tags.

Addressing this research challenge, in this paper we present an algorithm that is aimed at predicting user-tags from the associated textual metadata. Despite significant research developments in the area of video processing towards semantic tagging, much of these techniques are bounded to the a-priori knowledge of the video domain. Since, by nature Internet videos are not bounded to anything particularm, and could potentially range from sports or software tutorials to religious lectures, we considered textual metadata to provide a more reliable source of information which does not require the need for training based on a-priori knowledge. Therefore, the associated textual information is identified as a rich source of information for extracting high-level semantics. However, in order to effectively and efficiently index these media items, the free-text description needs to be analysed and corresponding tags with semantic meaning should be extracted. From the analysis of the associated descriptions, we realised that authors in general provide a summary of the video content along with briefly contextualising the video, and these textual metadata often contains specific references to places, people and other related semantic information commonly referred to as named entities. Hence, our approach is based on exploiting the complementary resources such as Wikipedia and Wordnet in order to extract semantically meaningful tags from a largely unstructured textual resource. To this end, we developed a user-tag prediction framework in which the GATE NLP tools for named entity extraction are utilised. The proposed framework has been tested in the "MediaEval2010 Tagging Task", more specifically, for both "closed set" and "open set" annotation of internet videos. For effective performance evaluation of the framework, a filename-based classifier has been developed as an additional source for predicting video tags.

The rest of the paper is organised as follows. In Section 2, an overview of the named entity recognisers are briefly presented folowed by rationale for choosing "Wikipedia" as a source of information in Section 3. Section 4 outlines in details the proposed extension to the GATE NLP framework along with the developed Bag-of-Article (BOA) classifier. In addition, alternative methods used in the evaluation of predicting user-tags has been briefly outlined in Section 5. Finally the evaluation results are presented in 6 which is followed by conclusion and future work in Section 7.

2   Related Research

Most research in this field has so far focused on non-statistical approaches, particularly on the lexico-syntactic patterns (Hearst patterns) first introduced in [1]. While purely statistical approaches such as Latent Semantic Indexing (LSI) are prevalent in other fields of natural language processing, until recently they were only suitable for discovering symmetrical relations between words. The closest task to hypernym discovery mentioned in the seminal text book on statistical natural language processing [2] is unsupervised disambiguation, in which k meanings of a term are determined automatically. This approach has however the limitation that meaning is not represented by a single word (term) but by a context. Recent research [3] introduced one of the first statistical methods to hypernym discovery. Their work utilizes Principal Component Analysis (PCA) for discovering term taxonomies (hierarchies of hypernyms). The algorithm presented here is closest to the research of Cimiano et al [4], who use lexico-syntactic patterns also codified in a JAPE transducer grammar. The focus is however different, their framework Text2Onto tries to learn the whole ontology, while the work presented here tries to discover only hypernyms for the given query.

Query expansion is probably the most typical application of hypernym (taxonomy) discovery. Query expansion is a method for improving recall and possibly the precision of information retrieval by expanding the query with other terms related to the original query. These terms are usually weighted. Query expansion has not been found to provide any significant objective improvement, although it is perceived positively by the users [5], [6]. Query refinement is a related technique that essentially recommends new terms that replace the original query or lengt- hen it. In practice, a user typically types a search query and then the search results are shown with possible new refined queries. Query refinement alone suffers from several problems. Particularly, the user cannot easily compare two candidate refinements as the result totally changes when he/she clicks on the refined query. In our research, we use hypernyms for query refinement. Refined queries are, however, used for on-the-fly clustering of search results rather than for giving the user the opportunity to issue a new query. Clustering does not suffer from the above-mentioned problem of query refinement as the user sees all the refinements on one screen.

3   Wikipedia as the Source of Knowledge

A gold standard dataset for training and testing hypernym discovery algorithms is WordNet ([7], [8]). WorldNet has structured nature and general coverage makes it a good choice for general disambiguation tasks. The focus of work presented here is on specialized domain (the test domain is football), which makes the use of WordNet less appealing. Most existing lexical resources including WordNet will have difficulty finding hypernyms for specialized search queries such as the name of a footballer or football arena. In experiments with automatically learned rather than hand-crafted lexico-syntactic patterns [8], using TREC dataset and Wiki- pedia as the training corpus gave a significant improvement to the best WordNet classifier (F-Measure from 0.2339 to 0.3592).

Our previous work relied on WordNet thesaurus [9], but it turned not to be exhaustive enough and we decided to search for another source of information.

In this sense Wikipedia turned out to be convenient as we needed a closed corpus of texts where the duplicity of articles describing the distinctive semantic category of the given word is minimal. In this regard the general web cannot serve as a good source while Wikipedia tries to cover most of the semantic meanings using only limited number of pages (usually only one page). Therefore, we found the first section of Wikipedia articles as particularly suitable for hypernym discovery and use it as the sole source of information.

4   Overview of the Proposed Framework

The proposed framework consists of two stages. The first stage is the tag pre-processing where each tag from the list of all tags is processed and further expanded if needed. The algorithmic workflow is presented in Figure 1. As tags in general can contain any keyword which the author might consider as relevant, it was important to contextulise the tags. To this end, the pre-processing framework developed is aimed at categorising the tags into two general categories, namely, (i) common tags and (ii) named entity tags. Common tags are those which correspond to either an action, country or as depicted in the figure have a synset associated to it in WordNet. On the other hand, named entity tags are those tags which do not have a WordNet synset and depends on external resources to contextulise them. The objective of this pre-processing is to ensure that named entity tags are disambiguated enough to enable a match semantic similarity search.

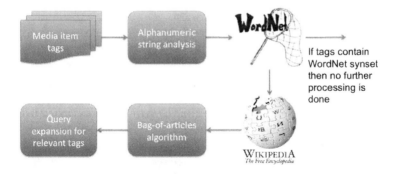

Fig. 1. Overview of the tag pre-processing phase

An overview of the second stage of processing is presented in Figure 2. As we considered the metadata (i.e. video title, video description, automatic speech recognition (ASR) transcripts) to be of value in determining the nature of tags, we first processed the metadata with GATE[1] NLP framework. The framework includes a tokeniser, sentence splitter, and Part-of-Speech (POS) tagger. In addition to the basic text components, we also included a Gazetteer in order to

---

[1] http://gate.ac.uk/

identify entity names in the text based on lists of predefined words. Also, for extraction of additional semantic information we included the Java Annotation Pattern Engine (JAPE) to extract hypernyms from Wikipedia. Finally, we also included OpenCalais[2] plugin for extraction of named entities from the textual metadata.

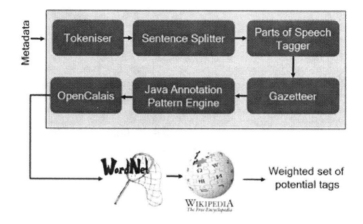

Fig. 2. Overview of the proposed system

One of the significant contributions of this paper is the integration of Bag-of-Articles (BOA) algorithm in to the framework as an extension to GATE NLP tools. Briefly, the module locates a Wikipedia article using the unlabeled entity through media wiki API. The similarity measure for determining the article's relevance to the tag is obtained through text relevance with popularity of the articles [10]. From the selected article, a JAPE implementation of Hearst patterns was used to extract a hypernym. This hypernym was then looked up in Wordnet, thus establishing a link between the entity and a Wordnet synset.

As previously mentioned, Wikipedia presents a much larger data resource compared to Wordnet for named entity extraction such as people, places, organisation and events to name a few. In order to exploit Wikipedia resources, the BOA classifier has been developed. The proposed BOA is an extension of the well-known Bag-of-Words (BOW) approach [11]. The input for the BOA classifier is the classified entity represented as a noun chunk and a set of class entities, represented with a Wikipedia page title. For unlabeled entities, the BOA classifier locates articles in Wikipedia that might define the entity and selects one of them using a disambiguation function. Subsequently, it uses link analysis to try to identify related articles falling into the same semantic category, and then creates a BOA term weight vector by aggregating their BOWs vectors. The class is assigned by choosing the closest class entity, also a BOA term weight vector, with cosine similarity or other suitable metric.

---

[2] http://www.opencalais.com/

4.1   Bag-of-Articles Classifier

Formally, the input of a BOA classifier is a set of t labeled instances (titles of Wikipedia articles) C and a set of u unlabeled instances (noun phrases) E. Wikipedia article titles provide an unanimous mapping between the labeled instance and a Wikipedia article. We use symbol W to denote a collection of all pages in Wikipedia at a given time. Each article is described by its title, term weight vector, outbound links, a list of categories it belongs to and type (article page, disambiguation page, category page,...). The BOA representation, as proposed here, does not process Wikipedia infoboxes.

For an unlabeled instance $e_x \in E$, it is first necessary to determine the articles that may be defining its various senses. The ranking function ρ maps it onto the vector of its n possible senses $s_x = \rho(e_x, W) = \langle s_{x,1} \ldots s_{x,l} \ldots s_{x,n} \rangle$. The senses – titles of Wikipedia *article pages* – are sorted in the vector in the decreasing order of relevance. The sense l of an unlabeled instance e_x is represented by article title $s_{x,l}$. The fact that there are multiple senses for the unlabeled instance gives space for disambiguation function δ. In the base scenario, we use disambiguation function δ_{mfs}, which assigns the most frequent sense:

$$\delta_{mfs}(s_x) = s_{x,1}. \tag{1}$$

Now, both a disambiguated unlabeled instance and a labeled instance is a Wikipedia article title and can be mapped to a Wikipedia article. In the following, we will use the variable a to refer to a Wikipedia article to which an instance (labeled or unlabeled) is mapped. The bag of articles $\beta(a)$ is constructed by aggregating related article across the set of modalities M with the help of the modality membership function μ, article term-weighting function τ and recursive term-weight aggregation function θ.

Modality membership μ. Modality membership function $\mu(a, a_r) \mapsto \{0, 1\}$ expresses if article a_r is considered related to a ($\mu = 1$) or not ($\mu = 0$). Several modality membership functions are suggested below. Article a is evaluated as related to a_r ($u \neq u_r$) if

- $\mu_{outlink}(a, a_r) = 1$ iff a links to a_r,
- $\mu_{backlink}(a, a_r) = 1$ iff a_r links to a,
- $\mu_{related\ outlink}(a, a_r) = 1$ iff a links to a_r and there is an article a_c linking to a and a_r, $a_r \neq a \neq a_c$,
- $\mu_{backlinking\ outlink-firstpara}(a, a_r) = 1$ iff a links to a_r, a_r links to a and the link from a to a_r is contained in the first paragraph of a,
- $\mu_{shared\ category\ outlink}(a, a_r) = 1$ iff a links to a_r and a and a_r share the same category.

Other modality membership function definitions are also possible and various have been in fact suggested in the literature, albeit under a different name. This applies e.g. to $\mu_{backlinking\ outlink-firstpara}$ [12] or $\mu_{related\ outlink}$, which is used in the Lucene Search Mediawiki Extension (refer to Section 4.1). We use the symbol $A^a_{\mu_m}$ to denote the set of all articles a_r that are related to a with respect to modality membership function μ_m:

$$A^a_{\mu_m} = \{a_r | a_r \in W, \mu_m(a, a_r) = 1\}. \tag{2}$$

Article term-weighting τ. The weight function $\tau(a) \mapsto R^n$ represents the article a as a vector of term weights. The parameter $w_{m,d}$ is a weight assigned to term vectors $\tau(a)$ in modality m and depth d. The term weight functions considered are:

- term frequency (TF),
- term frequency - inverse document frequency (TF-IDF) computed over entire Wikipedia,
- term frequency - inverse document frequency computed over articles included in bag of articles of labeled instances C,
- term frequency with first paragraph[3] boost.

Other term-weight function definitions can be also considered.

Recursive term-weight aggregation θ. The function $\theta_m(a, d, maxd_m) \to R^n$ recursively aggregates term-weight vectors of articles related to a according to the modality membership function μ_m:

$$\theta_m = \begin{cases} \sum_{a_r \in A^a_{\mu_m}} [w_{m,d}\, \tau(a_r) + \theta_m(a_r, d+1, maxd_m)] & \text{if } d < maxd_m \\ 0 & \text{if } d = maxd_m. \end{cases} \tag{3}$$

Bag of articles β. Function $\beta(a) \mapsto R^n$ creates the bag of articles for article a:

$$\beta(a) = \tau(a) + \sum_{m \in M} \theta_m(a, 1, maxd_d). \tag{4}$$

The formula aggregates the term-weight vector for article a with term-weight vectors of articles recursively related to it up to level $maxd_m$, $maxd_m \in N$. The articles (directly) related to it have level 1.

The classification is done by comparing the BOA vector of the unlabeled instance $\beta(a_x)$ with BOA term vectors of labeled instances $\beta(a_c)$ with the similarity metrics sim and selecting the class with the highest similarity:

$$BOAclass(a_x) = arg\ \max_c\ sim(\beta(a_x), \beta(a_c)). \tag{5}$$

A BOA classifier implementation needs to make decisions as of the selection of the ranking function ρ, modality membership functions μ_m, term weighting

---

[3] The first paragraph of a Wikipedia article contains usually the definition of the article subject, it can be therefore expected to contain more relevant words than the rest of the text.

function τ and the BOA similarity function *sim*. The weights $w_{m,d}$ and the maximum depth $maxd_m$ for gathering related pages in modality m are externally set. Except for the function *sim*, all these settings are made separately for labeled and unlabeled instances.

Implementation. This section describes an experimental implementation of the BOA-based classification system. As the ranking function ρ, the implementation uses a composite metric, which combines text-based similarity between the noun chunk and article text and article popularity as measured by the number of backlinks. As modality membership function μ_m, there is one option - *outlinks*, implementation of *backlinks* is in progress. For the term weighting function τ, there is a TF and TF-IDF support. As the BOA similarity metrics *sim*, the implementation uses cosine similarity.

A BOA classifier requires a Wikipedia index containing the following pieces of information about each article:

- term vectors with term frequencies,
- outlinks,
- popularity ranking (for mostfrequent sense relevance ranking).

Given the current size of English Wikipedia and the fact that it is constantly updated, meeting these data acquisition requirements results in a considerate engineering effort and in fact a reimplementation of an existing software as these functions are from the most part performed by the existing *Lucene-Search* Mediawiki Extension[4]. This *Lucene*[5]-based Mediawiki search engine indexes the Mediawiki article database and creates four Lucene indexes: the main index, the links index, the related index, the headlines index and spellcheck index. For the BOA classifier, the main index containing term vectors and the links index containing links leading out of each article are the most important. This extension provides two additional vital functions for the BOA classifier - parsing of wikitext and prospectively the ability to perform incremental updates.

The main `wiki` index contains the following important fields: `title`, `key` with a numeric article identifier, the term vectors are saved in the `contents` field, `category` stores article's categories, `related` stores titles of articles that were determined as related during indexing[6]. The `wiki.links` index contains the following fields: `Article key` containing concatenated article title, `Article PageID` with a unique numeric identifier that binds the entry with the main index `key` field, `links` with a list of article titles to which the article links. The index differentiates between different types of links (article/image) using a namespace (prefix), `redirect` contains the title of the article to which the current article is redirected, `rank` contains the number of backlinking articles. In the BOA classifier implementation, these indexes are exploited as follows.

---

[4] http://www.mediawiki.org/wiki/Extension:Lucene-search
[5] http://lucene.apache.org
[6] A is said to be related to B, if A links to B, and there is some C that links to both A and B (source: Lucene-Search Extension documentation).

Term vectors. Indexed Wikipedia articles are stored in the `wiki.main` index, however the Lucene-Seach extension does not store term vectors. For the purpose of the BOA classifier, it was necessary to modify the extension with code for storing the term vectors.

Outlinks. This information can be obtained from the `links` field of the article entry in the `wiki.links` index.

Popularity ranking. The Lucene-Search Extension contains a search engine, which uses sophisticated relevance ranking involving the number of backlinks. The BOA implementation uses the first-ranked article as the MFS baseline.

The Lucene Mediawiki Indexer as used in the BOA classifier system has several changes in code, the most marked one is the extension of the index with stored term vectors. The term vector computations are done with a *sparse matrix toolkit* java library[7].

5   Alternative Approaches for Predicting User-Tags

In order to have a fair evaluation of the proposed framework and as we couldn't find any related articles for predicting user-tags we developed the following two approaches to study the performance of different algorithms on the MediaEval 2010, Wild Wild Web (WWW) dataset. The first approach is based on expanding known entities with Wordnet and performs a similarity matching function by constructing TF/IDF matrix. The latter approach is based on the logical analysis of replicating the user-behaviour when assigning video file names to tagging online-videos.

5.1   Wordnet-Based Classification

In a conventional sense Wordnet resources have been exploited for disambiguation purposes. In this paper, for the evaluation of the proposed framework, we used the Lin similarity metric between the Wordnet synset representing an entity with each of the target tags. The Lin similarity measure has sound theoritical foundation stated in the Similarity Theorem [13] and is defined as

$$sim_L(c_1, c_2) = \frac{2 * log\, p(lso(c_1, c_2))}{log\, p(c_1) + log\, p(c_2)} \tag{6}$$

The function *lso* returns the lowest common subsumer from the hierarchy, and the value $-log(p(c))$ is called information content (IC). The value $p(c)$ denotes the probability of encountering an instance of concept c, which is estimated from frequencies from a large corpus. Our implementation uses the Java Wordnet Similarity Library[8] (JWSL), which automatically derives the values of IC from the Wordnet structure by exploiting the hyponymy relations among synsets. Entities for which no synset is found and/or they are categorized as "unknown", were further processed using a JAPE hypernym extraction system using Wikipedia as the corpus.

---

[7] http://code.google.com/p/matrix-toolkits-java/
[8] http://grid.deis.unical.it/similarity

5.2 Filename-Based Classification

As previously mentioned, this approach exploits the human reasoning behind naming video files and is aimed at transforming the user-behaviour towards predicting user-tags. In addition, the video file name contains intrinsic semantic information, in particular when multiple file names starting with or containing a major portion of the file name. This approach is based on the implementation of a filename based classifier for which the development set from MediaEval 2010 dataset was used as a training set. The file-name based classifier was developed based on Weka statistical signal processing library.

6 Evaluation

In this section, we present an overview of the evaluation methodology we adopted for the evaluation of the proposed framework with other alternate methods presented. The evaluation consists of two parts, namely "closed-set annotation" and "open-set annotation". On one hand, the objective of closed-set annotation is to predict user-tags only from a list of tags provided. Although it should be noted that there are no restrictions on the data domain. On the other hand, in the "open-set annotation" there are no restrictions assigned to the list of tags that could be associated with the media items. In the rest of the paper, a detailed analysis of experimental results from all algorithms presented until now is discussed in details.

6.1 Closed Set Annotation

For the closed-set annotation, the evaluation was treated as a retrieval problem and using the TRECVID evaluation tool, we obtained MAP measure for different runs.

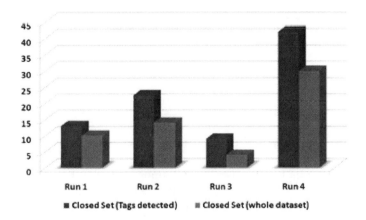

Fig. 3. MAP results from closed set annotation results

In Figure 3, although 1727 videos are present in the dataset, due to either the absence of title and/or description or the absence of named entities from these textual resources, tags were extracted only for 1671 videos. Therefore, the first set of evaluation namely "tags detected" was evaluated against the tags generated for 1671 videos and the second set of evaluation namely "whole dataset" was evaluated against the ground truth (tags for 1727 videos). The description of runs is as follows: run1 - includes ACR, video description and video title; run2 - includes only video description and video title; run3 - complete framework, run4 - filename based classifier.

6.2   Open Set Annotation

In order to provide a fair evaluation on the open-set annotation, we randomly selected 40 videos and had seven annotators to manually label if the tags associated to each video are "relevant" or "irrelevant". As a measure of relevance, we considered the "inter-annotator" agreement [3] among any three or more annotators and the results are summarized in Figure 4.

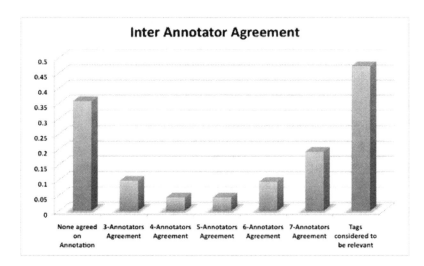

Fig. 4. Inter annotator agreement on the tags

A total of 296 tags were generated for the 40 videos considered for the evaluation and among them, 35.8% tags were considered to be irrelevant by all annotators. As shown in Figure 2, approximately 20% of the tags generated were considered to be relevant by all seven members of the annotators. Considering a tag with more than 3 inter-annotator agreement, then 47.3% of the tags generated were considered to be relevant and with 4 inter-annotator agreement, the percentage drops to 37.5%. For the total dataset of 1727 videos we obtained 6095 unique tags.

7   Conclusion and Future Work

In this paper a framework for predicting user-tags has been presented. The framework is an extension of the GATE NLP tools and furthermore the Bag-Of-Article is an extension of Bag-Of-Words. The performance analysis of the results for closed set annotation shows that filename based classifier outperforms the proposed framework. This indicates that a filename can be used as a strong tag predictor. On the other hand, proposed framework proved successful on the open-set annotation with almost 40% generated tags being considered relevant by 4 out of 7 manual annotators. The future work will focus on developing multi-modal techniques for effectively combining visual features and with file-named based classifier.

Acknowledgements. The research was partially supported by the European Commission under contract FP7-216444 PetaMedia.

References

1. Hearst, M.: Automatic acquisition of hyponyms from large text corpora. In: Fourteenth International Conference on Comput. Linguistics, pp. 539–545 (1992)
2. Manning, C., Schütze, H.: Foundations of Statistical Natural Language Processing. MIT Press (1999)
3. Bast H., Dupret G., Majumdar D., Piwowarski B.: Discovering a Term Taxonomy from Term Similarities Using Principal Component Analysis. Semantic Web Mining (2006)
4. Cimiano, P., Völker, J.: Text2onto - A Framework for Ontology Learning and Data-Driven Change Discovery. In: Montoyo, A., Muñoz, R., Métais, E. (eds.) NLDB 2005. LNCS, vol. 3513, pp. 227–238. Springer, Heidelberg (2005)
5. Nemeth, Y., Shapira, B., Taeib-Maimon, M.: Evaluation of the real and perceived value of automatic and interactive query expansion. In: SIGIR (2006)
6. Shapira B., Taieb-Maimon M., Nemeth Y.: Subjective and objective evaluation of interactive and automatic query expansion. Online Information Review (2005)
7. Gong, Z., Cheang, C.W., Hou, U.L.: Web Query Expansion by WordNet. In: Andersen, K.V., Debenham, J., Wagner, R. (eds.) DEXA 2005. LNCS, vol. 3588, pp. 166–175. Springer, Heidelberg (2005)
8. Snow, R., Jurafsky, D., Ng, A.: Learning syntactic patterns for automatic hypernym discovery. In: NIPS (2005)
9. Nemrava, J.: Refining search queries using WordNet glosses. In: EKAW (2006)
10. Kliegr, T., Chandramouli, K., Nemrava, J., Svatek, V., Izquierdo, E.: Combining Captions and Visual Analysis for Image Concept Classification. In: Proceedings of the 9h International Workshop on Multimedia Data Mining (2008)
11. Kliegr, T.: Entity Classification by Bag of Wikipedia Articles. In: Doctoral Consortium, CIKM (2010)
12. Cucerza, S.: Large-scale named entity disambiguation based on Wikipedia data. In: Proc. of Joint Conference on Empirical Methods in Natural Language Processing and Computational Natural Language Learning (2007)
13. Budanitsky A., Hirst G.: Evaluating wordnet-based measures of lexical semantic relatedness. Comput. Linguist. (2006)

LivingKnowledge: A Platform and Testbed for Fact and Opinion Extraction from Multimodal Data

David Dupplaw[1], Michael Matthews[2], Richard Johansson[3], and Paul Lewis[1]

[1] University of Southampton, UK
{dpd,phl}@ecs.soton.ac.uk
[2] Barcelona Media, Spain
mikemat@yahoo-inc.com
[3] University of Trento, Italy
johansson@disi.unitn.it

Abstract. In this paper, we describe the work we are undertaking in producing a truly multimedia platform for the analysis of facts and opinions on the web. The system integrates the analysis of multimodal data (images, text and page layout) into a distributable platform that can be built upon for various applications. We give an overview of the natural language processing tools that have been developed for extracting facts and opinions from the textual content of articles, the image analysis techniques used to extract facts and to help support the opinions found in the contextually related written information, as well as other multimodal tools developed for the analysis of online articles. We describe two applications that have been developed as part of ongoing work of the LivingKnowledge project: the News Media Analysis application for the semi-automation of the work of a media analysis company and the Future Predictor application which allows exploration of claims that are made through time.

1 Introduction

Extraction of knowledge from multimodal data on the web is a challenging prospect as any articulations of knowledge are strongly influenced by diversity (e.g. cultural influences or geographical location). Also, facts that are expressed within information may be subject to biases that mean the facts are distorted due to the claimant's position on some axis of diversity. In the LivingKnowledge project we aim to enhance the current state of search and knowledge management on the web by advancing the use of sentiment or opinion analysis within applications that combine text and images.

To realise the goal of recognising bias within web articles, it is first necessary to have strong fact and opinion extraction algorithms that can work in synergy and at a web-scale.

In this paper we will describe the platform that we have developed that allows the extraction of facts and opinions from large-scale crawls of web multimedia

A. Moschitti and R. Scandariato (Eds.): EternalS 2011, CCIS 255, pp. 100–115, 2012.

with the aim of providing a basis on which bias and diversity-aware applications may be built. We begin by describing the platform and the functionality it provides to developers of analytical algorithms. We will then briefly give an overview of the natural language processing tools, the image analysis tools and the holistic analysis tools that we are using to extract facts and opinions on the testbed. Finally we will illustrate how these facts and opinions are being used in two applications that we are developing as part of our project.

2   Testbed Analysis Platform

2.1   Data Representation

The central task in a project such as ours is to create automatic systems that extract structured information from unstructured sources – textual documents and media. This is a process that gradually adds *annotation* to the data collection. As has been previously observed, the structure of the data annotation is best modeled as an *annotation graph*[1,7]: a graph of interconnected *annotation entities* containing pieces of data where the lowest-level entities are grounded in raw data. In addition, to facilitate modularization and conceptual organization, annotation entities are grouped into *annotation layers*.

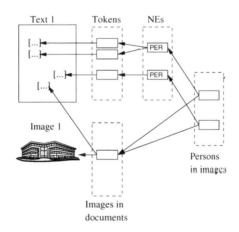

Fig. 1. Example of a graph of annotation entities over a data collection

Figure 1 shows an example of a collection of data and the representation of its annotations. The figure shows how complex annotation data – the connection between a person named in a document and an image, for example – is built on top of lower-level annotations: named entities (NEs), tokens (words), and image location annotation.

The platform has tools for dealing with the marshalling of this data into and out of an XML representation of this annotation graph. Annotation entities are given unique identifiers within the scope of the annotation file and may refer to other annotation types by reference to the document on which the annotations are made and a unique annotation type name. This allows annotations to have relations with other annotations thereby building the graphical representation. To maximise the openness of the annotation file format, each annotation may contain any structured information. Although this adds burden to modules wishing to reuse annotations, it means that no annotations are excluded from representation in the graph.

2.2   Testbed Architecture

To build bias aware applications, facts and opinions must first be extracted from the documents for which we are trying to determine bias. This requires a multitude of different multimodal extraction routines to be executed together on the same large set of documents and in a certain order to allow dependencies between analysis routines to be resolved.

To achieve this we have built the LivingKnowledge Testbed. It is a planned open source toolkit that allows for annotating document collections with analysis tools and provides methods for indexing, searching, and visualizing these annotations using the Solr search engine[1].

The major components of the testbed, shown in Figure 2, are the document collections, the annotation pipeline, the indexing and searching system, the provenance storage model and the evaluation framework.

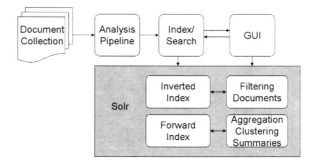

Fig. 2. Testbed Platform Architecture

The modular nature of the system allows for combining the analysis tools in different configurations and doing analysis on any document collection that has implemented a converter from the native collection format to the base annotation format. Modularisation of analysis algorithms is such that the algorithms can be written in any underlying programming language that is best for their implementation. Module execution is controlled by the testbed main core and allows

---

[1] http://lucene.apache.org/solr/

for the execution of modules in whichever order is necessary. Each module out-puts an annotation in XML that conforms to a defined annotation interchange format (see section 2.1).

As the testbed core is written in Java, any modules that are also written in Java can make use of tools that the core provides. The core provides automatic traversal of directories and documents and automatic parsing of the annotation interchange files. This means that the analysis code need not be bogged down with XML parsing functionality. External analysis modules are also supported by the testbed but these must marshal the annotation files themselves. In this way we have integrated Matlab, Python and native executables for analysing documents.

The testbed's analysis pipeline is internally divided into two - one pipeline specifically deals with analysis of images, while the main pipeline deals with the analysis of whole articles including their text. The rationale behind this is that individual images will have annotations that are not dependent on the context in which they appear (such as their colour distributions) and so these can be executed just once avoiding duplication. However, the images may also be analysed in the main pipeline in the context of the whole article allowing the image analysis routines to reduce their search space by utilising cues in the rest of the article (for example, recognition of faces that are mentioned within the article text).

One of the important parts of the testbed core is to extract information from the diverse set of document types that we encounter in various datasets to allow the analysis tools a consistent view of the incoming data. We have approached this problem with the use of the Apache Tika toolkit[2] which supports many common document formats, such as Word documents and PDFs, and converts their content into a consistent format that we subsequentally publish as a base annotation layer for the analysis tools. However, we found Tika was not accurate enough when extracting the information from web-pages: we found the output was cluttered with inconsequential words and images that appeared from the web-site template or decoration. Thus, we developed an HTML analysis tool that uses heuristics and an element voting mechanism that attempts to determine the important information from a cluttered page; that is, the main article text, the images which form part of the article (rather than decorative images), the main article title, section and sub-headings, links that form part of the article (rather than site navigation) and the article date. This tool has shown empirically that it is robust and extracts important information from many major online news and media outlets. The advantage of the tool is that the analysis algorithms will not, in the majority of cases, receive spurious text or images as their input, as text or images that appear in multiple pages on a single site (as navigation or decoration) are removed. This increases the accuracy of the analysis and, perhaps more importantly, the accuracy of any dataset summarisation. It has an additional advantage that it determines the important co-lateral text for images.

---

[2] http://tika.apache.org/

The testbed core also provides the automatic generation of provenance graphs for analysis chains. These graphs are generated and represented in the standard Open Provenance Model[3] (OPM) and injected into the analysis output as OPM XML in the annotation interchange format. After the analysis is complete, these graphs can be merged at the application level to produce a graphical representation of the complete analysis trail such as that shown in Figure 3. It allows an application to have a provenance of where a particular final annotation was constructed from and to be able to trace the value back through the annotation layers to the original document.

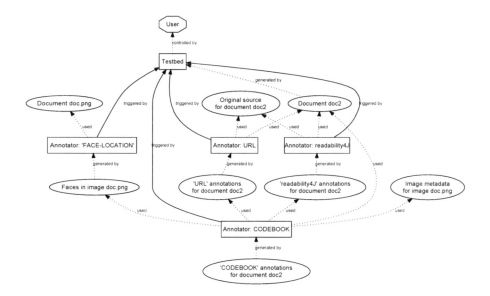

Fig. 3. Provenance graph for an analysis trail automatically generated by the testbed

The integration of image and text analysis tools in the same framework facilitates the creation of annotations based on input from diverse media formats. A simple XML format is used to control which document collection to use, which text and image analysis tools to apply and to specify which resulting annotations should be made available for search.

The testbed additionally provides an evaluation framework for measuring the performance of the system components against gold standard data. For each annotation module, a gold standard set is provided such that the module's performance can be automatically tested against the set via a standard cross-validation procedure. For annotations where fuzzy matches are necessary (such as image feature vector comparisons), plugin distance calculation functions can be written and re-used within the framework.

---

[3] http://openprovenance.org

In order to process large numbers of documents, we have created a Hadoop mapper tailored to processing the documents on a Hadoop cluster. Using 100 machines on a Hadoop cluster we are able to process millions of documents per day. The independent nature of the document processing means that the document throughput will increase linearly as the number of machines are increased.

Finally, there are various HTML visualization components that have been designed specifically to highlight the types of annotations provided by the analysis tools. Currently, the testbed supports several different document collections including the New York Times Annotated Collection[4], the MQPA dataset, BBN collection[5] and the Internet Archive (ARC) format[6]. Furthermore, there are visualization components included that support trends over time, facet aggregation, and facet correlations.

3   Extracting Facts and Opinions

Before axes of diversity, and hence bias, can be detected in articles, individual subjective and factual "objects" must first be extracted which can then be aggregated to form an overall view of the article. These "objects" may be explicit in the form of a claim in the text although they may also be somewhat more nebulous and only hinted at with specific use of imagery or juxtaposition of layout elements. It is therefore necessary to analyse not only the written text within an article, but also other elements such as images.

Below we briefly describe some of the modules that we have developed and used within the testbed platform for fact and opinion extraction. Firstly, we give an overview of the natural language processing that we use to extract explicit subjective statements from text within the page. We will then describe the image analysis and holistic page-based techniques that we aim to use to support or oppose the subjectivity that is being extracted from the textual content. By combining these analyses, we gather a more complete view of the context in which the claims are being expressed.

3.1   Text Analysis

The LivingKnowledge project aims to find expressions of *opinions* and track their diversity and evolution. The opinion analysis functionality in the LivingKnowledge platform consists of two parts: a very fast *coarse-grained* opinion extractor that finds sentences containing some expression of opinion, and a *fine-grained* system that extracts detailed information about the opinions: the person holding the opinion, whether the opinion is positive or negative (polarity), and the intensity of the opinion.

---

[4] http://www.ldc.upenn.edu/Catalog/CatalogEntry.jsp?catalogId=LDC2008T19
[5] http://www.ldc.upenn.edu/Catalog/CatalogEntry.jsp?catalogId=LDC2005T33
[6] http://www.archive.org/web/researcher/ArcFileFormat.php

Linguistic Processing. The fact and opinion analysis functionality is built on top of the information that we extract using a chain of natural language processing tools. As a first step, we apply the OpenNLP tool[7] to split the raw text into sentences and tokens and to assign a part-of-speech tag to each token. We extract named entities and coarse-grained word sense tags using the SuperSense tagger[2]. Grammatical and shallow semantic structures[10] are extracted by the LTH-SRL tool[9]. Finally, we use the TARSQI Toolkit[8] for annotating the temporal expressions in the document in the TimeML format[9].

Coarse-Grained Opinion Analysis. For processing large quantities of text, we apply a very fast classifier to quickly extract sentences containing some expression of opinion. Following earlier work in coarse-grained opinion analysis, we frame the problem of finding opinionated sentences as a *text categorization* problem: assigning every sentence to the category of subjective or objective. This allows us to apply well-established techniques for text categorization[6] using a bag-of-words representation of the sentences[11]. In addition to the words, we added extra features for words listed in a lexicon of common subjective words[17]. The classifier is implemented as a linear support vector machine that we trained using LIBLINEAR[4].

Fine-Grained Opinion Analysis. While the coarse-grained opinion extractor allows us to find opinionated sentences in text, many applications require more detailed information about the opinion, such as identifying the entity holding the opinion and determining its polarity and intensity. This analysis is carried out by the fine-grained opinion analysis system[8], which we implemented as a sequence of statistical systems trained on the MPQA dataset[10]. The representation used in MPQA is based on the psychological theory of private states[16]. The core concept in this representation is the *opinion expression*: a piece of text that makes us understand that some entity (such as an individual or organization) has a feeling towards some subject.

The system consists of four components:

- a sequence labeler that finds opinion expressions,
- an opinion holder extractor finds the entity holding the opinion,
- a classifier that determines the polarity of the opinion (positive, neutral, or negative),
- a classifier that determines the intensity of the opinion (low, medium, or high).

---

[7] http://opennlp.sourceforge.net
[8] http://www.timeml.org/site/tarsqi/
[9] http://www.timeml.org/site/index.html
[10] http://www.cs.pitt.edu/mpqa/databaserelease

3.2 Image Analysis

We believe that analysing images within articles can provide some hooks that will strengthen or weaken the opinions that are more explicitly stated within the text of the article.

High level image understanding has yet to be solved in the general case except for some specific application areas where the concepts can be more readily extracted. So it seems pertinent that we may utilise these existing higher-level analysis techniques where we can extract "facts" from the image which we can then interpret in the context of the article. For example, face detection and recognition have well established implementations that are relatively robust[18] and we have developed modules that we are training on politicians that we expect to see in the news crawls we are analysing.

It is very difficult to infer whether a standalone image is intended to harbour a sentiment and subsequentally influence the reader's opinion[20] due to the implicit nature of the concepts that are expressed within the image. However, it has been shown in [14] that colour features (spatial colour histograms) correlate with sentiment by crawling Flickr for images with tags containing words with negative or positive connotations from SentiWordNet and training a classifier: blue colours show negative connotations as compared to reds and yellows that are positive. Similarly, certain interest point features, like SIFT, have also been shown to correlate although the intuition is less obvious than the colour features. These correlations may show attempts to influence the reader's opinion on the subject depicted in the article.

We could, for example, combine these analyses with the text analysis of the article to find people in the image that match actors in the article text. Coupled with sentiment analysis of the image this may help to confirm opinions extracted from the text. For example, suppose the text of an article is found to be negative about Barack Obama and positive about John McCain and we are able to identify Obama in an associated image and that the image has negative sentiment values, then we see that the image supports or helps to confirm the interpretation from the text.

Conversely, we may be able to determine information about the image from it's textual context. On the web, images will have co-located text, either in explicit captions that appear in a visual cluster with the image (we can determine this by page analysis) or by the relative placement of the image within the main article. Analysing this text can provide some evidence towards the intended meaning of the image; if the claimant's opinion in the text is negative, an inference we make is that the image is illustrating that opinion. Using the graph-theoretic dominant set clustering algorithm, we annotate images with sentiment scores from SentiWordNet[11][19]. The essence is that we extract important sentiment words or phrases from the collateral text of images in the training set and organise the images around these categories. Each category is clustered using the dominant

---

[11] http://sentiwordnet.isti.cnr.it/

set clustering algorithm. Images for which we wish to obtain a sentiment score are placed in the feature space and are annotated with the category in which the nearest appears.

However, we have to be aware that co-located text may not be of the same opinion as the image. For example, the author's intended association may be for contrast and deliberately juxtaposed in opinion. When this is considered, it becomes a very difficult task to attempt to determine the intended sentiment behind an image.

In the project we are also investigating image forensics. It must be assumed that for specific types of image manipulations, the author of the image intended to project a particular opinion by using the manipulations. Manipulations such as face or sub-image replacement can be detected[12] and clearly indicate an attempt to influence opinion. Image alterations such as brightness and contrast enhancement can also be detected which may indicate an attempt to project an opinion; for example, a more colourful and vibrant visual may be associated with an intent to project a positive opinion.

3.3   Page Layout Analysis

Determining which images are related to which parts of the article text is an important analysis step to ensure that appropriate correlations are made. The HTML analyser that the testbed provides will ensure that only the important images are passed on for analysis, however, the positioning of those images within the page determines what text is co-located. To find this out, we must render web-pages in a controlled browser environment because alterations made by cascading style sheets can mean that page elements are drawn in places that the HTML alone would not make apparent. Text block elements that are both near an image and part of the main article text are marked as being co-lateral text for that image. It may be possible to go further with the analysis of a page at the structural or layout level and we are currently investigating whether web-sites that are more prone to bias in general (for example, websites of tabloid newspapers versus broad-sheet newspapers) have particular layout features. This requires determining features vectors that represent the page layout as a whole such as the area ratio of visual versus textual elements or determining types of header layout and size.

4   Multimedia Applications

The goal of creating a platform that provides web-scale multimodal analysis of web-based articles is to improve the user experience in knowledge retrieval applications. Clearly, the range of such applications is unfathomable, so the project has applied the system to two main application case studies which are designed to show how automatically annotating articles with opinion-led features can help particular tasks as well as producing new and interesting services. The applications we have built on top of the analysis platform aim to show these two advances.

4.1   Media Content Analysis

In modern media societies, public communication is very often mediated in a technical sense and the research carried out to facilitate such communication is focussed on what mediated public discourse concerning particular topics looks like. Media Content Analysis (MCA) methods can be used to study *trends* in public perceptions and the *impact* of some particular event, policy, or media strategy on the media discourse. By analysing written text and photographs from different webpages, an attempt is made to address the question of who says what to whom with what interest and in which channel. This is done by formulating the analysis on a hierarchy of domain, article, claims (or statements), subject actors, addressees, object actors, issues and frames. For each of these levels, a codebook is conceptualised in order to capture indicators and variables at each of the levels. These *codings* are populated by a human (the *coder*) who looks behind the article, inquires into the social reality and nonmanifest context that is being constructed by an article's manifest, written text and other meaningful matters. While this approach requires a deep reading of the article, automatic methods have a large potential to speed up this process and there is consequently a long history of computer-assisted MCA. However, these analysis tools have generally been based on simple word-spotting techniques, such as the famous General Inquirer system[15] and there is obviously a need to study the feasibility of applying modern methods in automatic text and multimedia analysis instead.

With our Media Content Analyser application we provide a web-based system to enhance the research goals of the human coders who are coding an article. Enhancements are provided in the form of automatic coding of fields or sets of fields within the coding sheet that represents the article. These are inferred or generated by the underlying analysis modules that exist in the testbed. A special module in the testbed takes the results of the text and image analysis modules and outputs a coding sheet which can then be used by the web-based application. Although this is batch-mode analysis of articles (rather than on-demand analysis), it means that it is possible to scale the analysis to web-scale and using a customised search engine to select articles to code. This allows much better coverage by providing better selection of appropriate articles to code than the the the current method where articles must be searched for by hand.

The automatic extraction of subjective statements (described above in section 3.1) is used to suggest to the coder possible statements that they may wish to add to the codebook. The coder can choose one of the extracted statements and a new coding sheet will be generated that has been automatically completed with the information available from the extracted statement such as the claimant, the addressee, or the time and date it was made. This is clealy a time-saving measure as the coder can use the automatically extracted list to get an overview of the statements made in the article without concern of missing any. We are currently evaluating the accuracy and usefulness of the extracted statements against a manually coded ground-truth set.

Clearly, the introduction of coding support by the insertion of automatic codings into the coding sheet is good for productivity. An important aspect of the application is that any automatic information codings have their provenance stored and made available for viewing. Tracing the source of certain codings allows the human coder to build trust in certain automatic codings. The testbed has been built so that Open Provenance Model (see section 2) graphs are automatically stored alongside annotations (see Figure 3). When annotators are able to provide confidence values for the automatic annotations, these can be also presented to the coder such that they can make an informed decision about whether to accept the provided field value. Indeed, it is possible to reduce the coder's work by avoiding the verification step and automatically confirming field values that have been derived from annotations that have high confidence values.

The hierarchical nature of the coding sheets means that higher-level sheets can be shared between coders. For example, the very top-level *domain* coding sheet contains indicators and variables that are specific to the article publisher (e.g. the online news site). As this is static for all articles from that publisher, this only need be filled in once, saving time for subsequent coding tasks.

The coding sheets are also augmented with semantic information; that is, some of the indicators within a coding sheet must contain specific conceptual types. The codebook that is used to generate the coding sheets is defined in XML and allows for fields to be given specific data types. These are URIs and so may refer to any conceptual entity on the linked open data cloud. We have created a web-service that automatically augments the web-article with URIs for conceptual entities in RDFa. The entities are matched against available entities

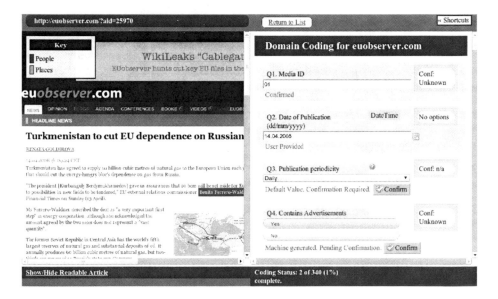

Fig. 4. Media Content Analysis Application

within ontologies (currently we're using DBPedia[12]) and the service returns an XHTML+RDFa version of the original page. The MCA application then uses the RDFa information to highlight entities and form links between the coding sheet variables and the displayed entities in the article.

Figure 4 shows a screenshot of the web-based MCA application. The left-hand side of the application displays the original article augmented with the RDFa tags. The right-hand side of the application displays the coding sheet.

4.2   Future Predictor

The Future Predictor builds on all of the analysis tools to give users a glimpse into the future. The first prototype of the system, the Time Explorer, was designed to enable the users to understand how news stories evolve over time and how they might evolve. Time Explorer was developed using the New York Times Annotated Corpora[13] and the output of a subset of the analysis tools available in the testbed including OpenNLP, the SuperSense tagger and the TARSQI Toolkit. The resulting analysis is used to extract from each document all of the person, location and organization entities and all time expressions that can be resolved to a specific day, month or year. The temporal expressions extracted are both explicit as in "September 2010" and relative as in "next month". The relative dates are resolved based on the **publication date** of the article and all dates are associated as **event dates** with the corresponding documents.

From these extractions, two indices are created, one for each document in the collection and one for each sentence in the collection. For the sentence level index, a **content date** is computed as one or more of the **event dates** found in the document or the **publication date** if there are no event dates. For example, given the following hypothetical document with publication date of May 1st, 1999:

> Slobodan Milošević became president of Yugoslavia in 1997. Slobodan Milošević will run for president again next year.

Fig. 5. Searching the Future of Iraq

Two sentences will be found. *Slobodan Milošević* will be extracted as a person in both sentences and *Yugoslavia* will be extracted as a location in the first sentence. *1997* will be extracted as a time expression in the first sentence and *next year* will be extracted as an expression in the second sentence and resolved to 2000. The **publication date** for both sentences will be May 1st, 1999 while the **content date** of the first sentence will be 1997 and the **content date** of the second sentence will be 2000. The resulting indices can be used to construct

---

[12] http://www.dbpedia.org/

very powerful queries, including queries about possible future events. For example, Figure 5, shows the results for a search on *Iraq* which allows for looking at predictions such as the one shown suggesting that Iraq could develop missiles capable of hitting the U.S by 2015. The Future Predictor builds on Time Explorer by incorporating the opinion-based annotations provided both on the text and images. In order to take advantage of images, it is necessary to move from the NYT corpus to a corpus that contains both text and images. For this, we have custom crawled a set of 7 million documents including associated images focused around European elections. Adapting the Future Predictor to make use the new corpus and incorporate new annotations is a simple matter of changing the configuration XML file to point to the new corpus and adding the opinion annotators to the pipeline.

Fig. 6. Snippet for query on Russia with negative image associated

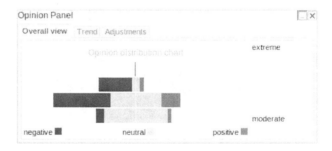

Fig. 7. Opinion Summary for Iraq

To take advantage of these changes required some additional visualization components specific to the opinion extraction and images. The primary visualization summarizes both the polarity and intensity dimensions of opinion for a given query as shown Figure 7 which aggregates the opinions for the query Iraq. The user is able to drill into documents that contain a particular type of opinion by clicking on the appropriate part of the graph. This combination of features allows the user to both see the aggregate opinion on a particular query, and also to quickly view documents reflecting a particular opinion. Finally, there is trend view of the opinions that allows users to view how opinions evolve over time and allows them to drill into periods of interest. Images with positive and negative sentiment are associated with the corresponding documents and thus can be incorporated in document summaries on the result page to provide a visual summary of content that compliments the textual summary. For example, Figure 6 displays a snippet generated for a document matching a query for documents containing the keyword Russia containing negative images. This document is discussing the cost of a gas war between Russia and the Ukraine and the picture complements the summary by showing an empty gas vat. We plan on also integrating the bias aware components of the LivingKnowledge project to gain further insights into whether similar opinions are expressed across groups or if different groups express different opinions. In elections, for example, it would be interesting to note differences of opinion between left and right wing news sources on the future of important topics such as global warming, immigration and terrorism.

5   Conclusion

In this paper we have given an overview of the analysis platform that we have built as part of the LivingKnowledge project that is working towards building bias and diversity aware applications. We have described how the platform integrates diverse analysis tools and provides the analysis pipeline, the provenance model, the evaluation framework and the HTML analyser that extracts important text and images from articles. The testbed augments the platform with data that allows these analysis tools to be evaluated. While flexible infrastructures for text analysis application development have been developed previously, such as GATE [3] and UIMA [5], the LivingKnowledge platform is the first one to be explicitly designed with multimodality in mind and to seamlessly integrate text and image analysis into a single architecture. Unlike other frameworks, our platform is also program language agnostic.

We use the testbed to create applications to showcase both the testbed and the analysis modules for fact and opinion extraction. The natural language and image analysis modules take forward the research in their respective areas; in their overviews we have given pointers here to where the reader can find more information about this research. However, the aggregation of multimodal data, including holistic page analysis, is certainly a new and interesting way to look at information extraction and the MCA application and the Future Predictor applications, although still in development, already show promise in their use of this diverse data.

As the LivingKnowledge project continues to develop, we will begin to show that bias and diversity aware applications will improve the user experience when searching, analysing and presenting information from the web.

Acknowledgements. This work was supported by the European Union under the Seventh Framework project LivingKnowledge (IST-FP7-231126). We would also like to thank all our partners who contributed to the LivingKnowledge project on which this work has been built.

References

1. Bird, S., Liberman, M.: A formal framework for linguistic annotation. Speech Communication 33(1,2), 23–60 (2001)
2. Ciaramita, M., Altun, Y.: Broad-coverage sense disambiguation and information extraction with a supersense sequence tagger. In: Processings of the 2006 Conference on Empirical Methods in Natural Language Processing, Sydney, Australia, pp. 594–602 (2006)
3. Cunningham, H., Maynard, D., Bontcheva, K., Tablan, V.: GATE: A framework and graphical development environment for robust NLP tools and applications. In: Proceedings of the ACL (2002)
4. Fan, R.-E., Chang, K.-W., Hsieh, C.-J., Wang, X.-R., Lin, C.-J.: LIBLINEAR: A library for large linear classification. JMLR 9, 1871–1874 (2008)
5. Ferrucci, D., Lally, A.: UIMA: an architectural approach to unstructured information processing in the corporate research environment. Natural Language Engineering 10(3-4), 327–348 (2004)
6. Joachims, T.: Learning to Classify Text using Support Vector Machines. Kluwer/Springer (2002)
7. Johansson, R., Moschitti, A.: A flexible representation of heterogeneous annotation data. In: Proceedings of the Seventh conference on International Language Resources and Evaluation (LREC 2010), Valetta, Malta, pp. 3712–3715 (2010)
8. Johansson, R., Moschitti, A.: Reranking models in fine-grained opinion analysis. In: Proceedings of the 23rd International Conference of Computational Linguistics (Coling 2010), Beijing, China, pp. 519–527 (2010)
9. Johansson, R., Nugues, P.: Dependency-based syntactic–semantic analysis with PropBank and NomBank. In: CoNLL 2008: Proceedings of the Twelfth Conference on Natural Language Learning, Manchester, United Kingdom, pp. 183–187 (2008)
10. Palmer, M., Gildea, D., Kingsbury, P.: The proposition bank: An annotated corpus of semantic roles. Computational Linguistics 31(1), 71–106 (2005)
11. Pang, B., Lee, L., Vaithyanathan, S.: Thumbs up? Sentiment classification using machine learning techniques. In: Proceedings of the 2002 Conference on Empirical Methods in Natural Language Processing, Philadelphia, United States, pp. 79–86 (2002)
12. Rosa, A.D., Uccheddu, F., Costanzo, A., Piva, A., Barni, M.: Exploring image dependencies: a new challenge in image forensics. SPIE, vol. 7541, p. 75410X (2010), http://link.aip.org/link/?PSI/7541/75410X/1
13. Sandhaus, E.: The New York Times annotated corpus. Linguistic Data Consortium (2008)
14. Siersdorfer, S., Hare, J., Minack, E., Deng, F.: Analyzing and predicting sentiment of images on the social web. In: ACM Multimedia 2010, pp. 715–718. ACM (October 2010), http://eprints.ecs.soton.ac.uk/21670/
15. Stone, P.J., Dunphy, D.C., Smith, M.S., Ogilvie, D.M.: Associates: The General Inquirer: A Computer Approach to Content Analysis. MIT Press (1966)
16. Wiebe, J., Wilson, T., Cardie, C.: Annotating expressions of opinions and emotions in language. Language Resources and Evaluation 39(2-3), 165–210 (2005)
17. Wilson, T., Wiebe, J., Hoffmann, P.: Recognizing contextual polarity in phrase-level sentiment analysis. In: Proceedings of Human Language Technology Conference and Conference on Empirical Methods in Natural Language Processing, Vancouver, Canada, pp. 347–354 (2005)

18. Zhao, W., Chellappa, R., Phillips, P.J., Rosenfeld, A.: Face recognition: A literature survey. ACM Comput. Surv. 35, 399–458 (2003),
    http://doi.acm.org/10.1145/954339.954342
19. Zontone, P., Boato, G., Hare, J., Lewis, P., Siersdorfer, S., Minack, E.: Image and collateral text in support of auto-annotation and sentiment analysis. In: TextGraphs-5: Graph-based Methods for Natural Language Processing, pp. 88–92. The Association for Computational Linguistics (July 2010),
    http://eprints.ecs.soton.ac.uk/21514/
20. Zontone, P., Boato, G., Natale, F.G.B.D., Rosa, A.D., Barni, M., Piva, A., Hare, J., Dupplaw, D., Lewis, P.: Image diversity analysis: Context, opinion and bias. In: The First International Workshop on Living Web: Making Web Diversity a true asset, vol. 515, CEUR-WS (October 2009), http://eprints.ecs.soton.ac.uk/18168/

Behaviour-Based Object Classifier for Surveillance Videos

Virginia Fernandez Arguedas, Krishna Chandramouli, and Ebroul Izquierdo

Multimedia and Vision Research Group
School of Electronic Engineering and Computer Science
Queen Mary, University of London, Mile End Road, E1 4NS, London, UK
{virginia.fernandez,krishna.chandramouli,
ebroul.izquierdo}@eecs.qmul.ac.uk

Abstract. In this paper, a study on effective exploitation of geometrical features for classifying surveillance objects into a set of pre-defined semantic categories is presented. The geometrical features correspond to object's motion, spatial location and velocity. The extraction of these features is based on object's trajectory corresponding to object's temporal evolution. These geometrical features are used to build a behaviour-based classifier to assign semantic categories to the individual blobs extracted from surveillance videos. The proposed classification framework has been evaluated against conventional object classifiers based on visual features extracted from semantic categories defined on AVSS 2007 surveillance dataset.

Keywords: Object classification, geometrical models, surveillance videos, object tracking, motion features.

1   Introduction

Fully automatic object and event detection and classification is crucial in a society where surveillance systems are pervasive and monitored 24 hours a day. This is especially true in countries like UK where Norris and McCahill [1] has estimated to house more than 4.2M Closed Circuit Television (CCTVs). The ubiquitousness of CCTV cameras generates everyday a huge amount of data that is constantly supervised by humans for detecting abnormal activities. Human supervision would cause a huge need of resources as well as a huge dependency on surveillance officers. To mitigate the responsibilities of the surveillance officers, numerous computer vision techniques on object and event classification are proposed in the literature [2].

The techniques presented in the literature can be largely classified into two categories based on the features used to construct the classification model namely *appearance* and *object behaviour*. Appearance-based classifiers rely on the visual features as the main source of information for representing and recognizing objects, which includes features such as colour, texture and/or shapes [3,4]. However, these techniques are affected by the object size and resolution paving way

A. Moschitti and R. Scandariato (Eds.): EternalS 2011, CCIS 255, pp. 116–124, 2012.

towards sparsely represented problem. On the other hand, behaviour based classifiers exploit temporal and geometrical characteristics to distinguish between semantic categories. Geometrical features such as motion, spatial location and velocity are used to represent the object category's behaviour, providing information that is more robust to the common challenges encourted in surveillance video applications, for example changes in illumination, occlusions and/or shape distortion [5,6].

In this work, our goal is to present a novel set of geometrical features to define each object category's behaviour. Such geometrical features are extracted using object trajectories and further processed towards building a behaviour-based object classifier. The proposed technique offers invariance to external factors and general changes in the objects appearance. The proposed object classification approach procure a real time surveillance video analysis applied over realistic scenarios.

The rest of the paper is organised as follows. In Section 2, the proposed behaviour-based object classification framework is presented, followed by an analysis on the extraction of geometrical features in Section 3. The behaviour-based object classifier is briefly outlined in Section 4, as well as the evaluation results. Section 5 presents conclusions and some of the potential future work for the paper.

2   Object Classification Based on Geometrical Features

Our surveillance object classification approach is based upon extracting each object's geometrical features to compute its representation. The framework integrates three intermediate modules (as shown in Figure 1). First, a *Motion analisis component* is applied on the raw surveillance video to extract temporal evolution of blobs and motion features. Second, a set of novel geometrical features are calculated in an invariant view based extractor (see Section 3). Finally, a behaviour based object classifier is proposed exploiting the geometrical features previously extracted. The classifiers assigns labels to each blob from a set of pre-defined semantic labels considering the object behaviour rather than its appearance.

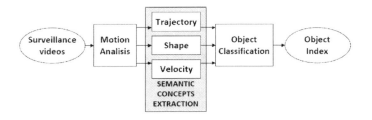

Fig. 1. The proposed behaviour-based object classifier framework

The first stage of the framework integrates the *motion analysis component*. The component aims to reduce the redundant information contained in surveillance videos [7]. This objective is fulfilled with the use of background substraction technique followed by spatial segmentation of moving objects and finally tracking the moving objects and assigning objects labels using Kalman filters. As a result, a set of bounding boxes, coordinates and temporal information have been extracted per each moving object that appeared in the surveillance video. This information is used subsequently to calculate the previously mentioned behavioural features. Despite the performance of the *motion analysis component*, several open challenges remain such as noisy and low quality images, lack of contrast or image blurring due to camera movement, as shown in Figure 2.

(a) Merge of blobs due to noisy images and shadows

(b) Appearance of new informationless blobs due to camera movement

Fig. 2. Effect of external factors over the objects appearance

3   Geometrical Features Extraction

For each object a temporal evolution set, corresponding to the coordinates and temporal information is obtained from the *Motion analysis component*. Object classifiers are based on the idea that objects can be represented by their appearance but also by their behaviour. However, while an object appearance might change for different reasons like a noisy image, changes in illumination, image blurring or other external factors, its behaviour model remains largely intact and often has shown to be invariant to previously mentioned problems.

All behaviour models are subjected to satisfy two necessary constraints: (i) a small intra-object variance and (ii) a high inter-object variance. In other words, features extracted should be highly representative of a given object category and at the same time easily distinguishable between different object categories. Extrapolation from realistic scenarios and from further analysis of surveillance dataset has led to the selection of a set of geometrical features whose patterns satisfied these constraints: *shape ratio*, *trajectory* and *velocity* (see Sections 3.2, 3.1 and 3.3 respectively).

Fig. 3. Different views of the same object, depending on the trajectory followed by the object its semantic concepts vary

The behavioural features are directly affected by object trajectory and also on the position of the camera, for instance, the object size varies if it is going away from the camera but remains constant if the object only passes by in perpendicular direction to the camera. Considering this, a pre-processing step, called *composed-trajectories division algorithm*, analyses each object trajectory and divides it into independent trajectories if any temporal and/or spatial breakpoints occur. A *temporal breakpoint* is considered when an object is stopped for a long time and therefore is more likely to change its direction. While a *spatial breakpoint* is a strong diversion in an object trajectory. Any of these *breakpoints* show a change in the trajectory, hence, a change in the object geometrical features (as shown in Figure 3). Every time a *breakpoint* is found, the object information is subdivided into two different and independent objects.

3.1 Trajectory

The main geometrical feature is *trajectory*. All the other concepts would rely on it in the rule-based analysis since *shape ratio* and *velocity* are trajectory-dependant measurements. Its calculation is directly related to *composed-trajectories division algorithm*, due to its calculation based on *trajectory angle*, θ, which is the basis to compute all the other measurements, where trajectory angle is:

$$\theta = atan\frac{\Delta y}{\Delta x} = atan\frac{|y_{t_2} - y_{t_1}|}{|x_{t_2} - x_{t_1}|} \tag{1}$$

Trajetory representation involves several measurements: (1) *trajectory angle*, calculated per object's sample $\theta = \{\theta_1, \theta_2, ..., \theta_{n-1}\}$, (2) *global trajectory angle* to describe the general movement of the object along time, (3) *vertical object directionality* to depict whether the object moves vertically or not, (4) *horizontal object directionality* to represent whether the object moves horizontally or not, (5) *quadrant* which is a condense depiction of the general directionality of the object's movement whose values are $1, 2, 3, 4$ as shown in Figure 4, (6) statistical measurements, which include maximum max_T, minimum min_T, average μ_T and standard deviation σ_T, to consider the variety of the object's samples within the object classification and indexing.

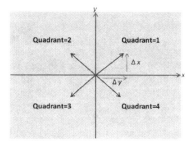

Fig. 4. Quadrant measurement scheme

3.2   Shape Ratio

After the application of the *composed-trajectories division algorithm*, each new object, B, is composed by a set of representations, $B = b_1, b_2, ..., b_n$ which have the same physical properties.

Shape ratio concept reflects not only the object general size but also its shape and proportion. The former is determined by the number of pixels composing the object's representation bounding box. While, the latter is pictured as the bounding box dimentions ratio. These geometrical features compute the behaviour of an object representation, in order to consider all the object's samples, several statistical measurements, which include maximum max_{SR}, minimum min_{SR}, average μ_{SR} and standard deviation σ_{SR}, are computed and considered as part of the object index.*Shape ratio* concept is highly dependant of the object trajectory and, therefore, dependant of its behaviour.

3.3   Velocity

Velocity feature procures a highly valuable information about the object category for classification in certain situations, i.e., when an object velocity overpasses a certain threshold, the object is classified as a car, due to the real-world physical constraints placed on the concept *Person*. However, there are ranges of values where object categories are not so easily distinguishable. For that reason, *velocity* feature is used to discard in case of ambiguity between concepts.

A geometric-based method is applied to calculate *velocity* feature. Considering each object, B, consists on a set of visual representations, $B = b_1, b_2, ..., b_n$, the geometric-based method follows the scheme shown in Figure 5 to calculate: (i) the visual distance between consecutive object's samples and (ii) the visual object velocity. To take all the object samples into consideration, several statistical measurements, which include maximum max_V, minimum min_V, average μ_V and standard deviation σ_V, are computed and considered as part of the object index.

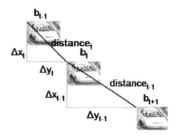

Fig. 5. Velocity calculation scheme

4   Experimental Results

The performance analysis of the proposed geometrical features is achieved by constructing a behaviour-based object classifier. First, the presented geometrical features are extracted and constitute the basis for the behaviour-based rule classifier. Since, each behaviour model depicts the object characteristics, a set of rule based membership functions are created. These membership functions are extrapolated from the marginal training sample created from the manually annotated dataset. The membership functions for different geometrical features have been calculated and are similar to one shown in Figure 6, calculated for *shape ratio*. In order to evaluate the performance of this object classification approach and the proposed geometrical features, behaviour-based object classification was applied to a variety of outdoor video sequences provided by IEEE International Conference on Advance Video and Signal based Surveillance, *AVSS 2007*.

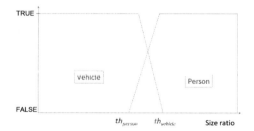

Fig. 6. Shape ratio membership function

Through a careful examination of the dataset, two object categories were noted to be highly repetitive in the sequences, namely *Person* and *Vehicles (or Car)*. The proposed object classifier categorises each extracted bounding box region as *person*, *vehicle* or *unknown* depending on its geometrical features and the behaviour model established in the object classifier. In order to study the efficiency of the proposed object classifier, a ground truth has been manually annotated. A total of 1376 objects were included, a 6% were person while a 94% were vehicle. Due to the imposed guidelines for the manual annotation and the challenges introduced by the motion analysis component, objects presenting certain constraints such as small blob size, partial occlusion of the object over a 50% or multiple objects coexisting in a blob, were annotated as *unknown*.

The proposed approach classifies objects depending on their behaviour model and is independent of the object's appearance. As previously stated behaviour features are extracted from the analysis of motion trajectory. *Velocity* feature provides a highly valuable information when an object overpasses a certain speed, however, in limited-speed roads, *velocity* cannot differentiate between object categories. Similarly, *Shape Ratio* feature considers not only the bounding box ratio but also the real size of the object. A fuzzy distance measure was assigned for the behaviour-based classifier to each object, to represent the certainty of the classifier. The experimental evaluation of the proposed behaviour-based classification is compared with appearance-based classification as depicted in Figure 8. However, prior to a comparative analysis, an evaluation of the discriminative power of the proposed geometrical features is shown in Figures 7(a),7(b). Figure 7(a) shows an average 35% performance for the concept *vehicle*, which outperforms in 20% the performance obtained for concept *person*. While for the feature *Size* (refer to Figure 7(b)), the concept *vehicle* outperforms the concept *person* in an average of 40%. The results obtained for *person* can be related to the sparseness of this object category within the ground truth, generating a less accurate model. On the other hand, the results for the concept *Vehicle*, generally exceed 30% and 35% for the geometrical features *shape ratio* and *size*, respectively. *Vehicle* results are limited for two reasons: (i) the road appearing in the surveillance video dataset has speed limitation and vehicles do not exceed person's speed and (ii) the appearance of vehicles with different silhouettes and shape ratios, some of them really similar to a person's shape ratio. The improvement of the anomalies between the interannotated agreements shows a 30% precision increase over 10% recall.

In [8], an exhaustive evaluation of appearance based feature study has been performed. In Figure 8, the presented behaviour-based object classifier is evaluated against an appearance-based object classifier built over multiple low-level visual primitives namely MPEG - 7 Colour Layout Descriptor, Edge Histogram Descriptor, Colour Structure Descriptor and Dominant Colour Descriptor. From the results presented in Figure 8, the behaviour-based models provide improved results for recall greater than 0.7. This characteristic is significant in case of both Vehicle/Car and Person. The results indicate the average performance of the multiple visual primitives from the appearance-based classifier. Similarly the behaviour-based feature model is an average of performance obtained on pixel and shape ratio features.

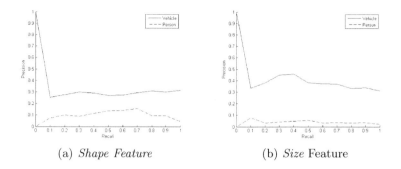

(a) *Shape Feature*   (b) *Size* Feature

Fig. 7. Retrieval performance of the *shape* and *size* features

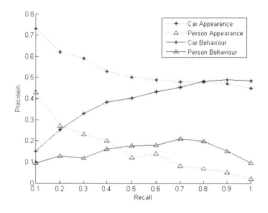

Fig. 8. Comparison of retrieval performance for appearance and behaviour based feature models

5   Conclusions and Future Work

In this paper, an investigation into the non-appearance based classification models is presented. The behaviour model based classifier is largely dependent on the motion trajectories exhibited by different objects, which are used to classify objects into semantic categories. The future work will focus on videos with non-speed-limited vehicles to be analysed to prove the importance of *velocity* concept for concept disambiguation. Moreover, a comprehensive object taxonomy will be developed to represent relationship between semantic categories. In addition, the object taxonomy will be formalised using semantic web languages to establish correlation with behavioural features with geometrical properties. Such an object representation is intended to enhance the inherent reasoning and inference process of the semantic media repositories containing surveillance videos.

Acknowledgments. The research was partially supported by the European Commission under contract FP7-SEC 261743 VideoSense.

References

1. McCahill, M., Norris, C.: Estimating the extent, sophistication and legality of CCTV in London. In: CCTV, pp. 51–66 (2003)
2. Piciarelli, C., Micheloni, C., Foresti, G.: Trajectory-based anomalous event detection. IEEE Transactions on Circuits and Systems for Video Technology 18(11), 1544–1554 (2008)
3. Schiele, B., Crowley, J.: Recognition without correspondence using multidimensional receptive field histograms. International Journal of Computer Vision 36(1), 31–50 (2000)
4. Pontil, M., Verri, A.: Support vector machines for 3D object recognition. IEEE Transactions on Pattern Analysis and Machine Intelligence 20(6), 637–646 (1998)
5. Bashir, F., Khokhar, A., Schonfeld, D.: Real-time motion trajectory-based indexing and retrieval of video sequences. IEEE Transactions on Multimedia 9(1), 58–65 (2007)
6. Javed, O., Shah, M.: Tracking and Object Classification for Automated Surveillance. In: Heyden, A., Sparr, G., Nielsen, M., Johansen, P. (eds.) ECCV 2002. LNCS, vol. 2353, pp. 343–357. Springer, Heidelberg (2002)
7. Stauffer, C., Grimson, W.: Learning patterns of activity using real-time tracking. IEEE Transactions on Pattern Analysis and Machine Intelligence 22(8), 747–757 (2000)
8. Fernandez Arguedas, V., Zhang, Q., Chandramouli, K., Izquierdo, E.: Multi-feature fusion for surveillance video indexing. In: 12th International Workshop on Image Analysis for Multimedia Interactive Services (April 2011)

Author Index

Baudry, Benoit   25
Bauer, Oliver   61
Ben David, Olivier-Nathanael   25
Bennaceur, Amel   79

Chandramouli, Krishna   88, 116
Corazza, Anna   42

Di Martino, Sergio   42
Dupplaw, David   100

Fernandez Arguedas, Virginia   116

Howar, Falk   61

Issarny, Valérie   79
Izquierdo, Ebroul   88, 116

Johansson, Richard   79, 100

Lamprecht, Anna-Lena   1
Lewis, Paul   100

Maggio, Valerio   42
Margaria, Tiziana   1
Matthews, Michael   100
Moschitti, Alessandro   34, 79

Neubauer, Johannes   61

Piatrik, Tomas   88

Saadi, Rachid   79
Sauer, Thomas   16
Scandariato, Riccardo   25
Scanniello, Giuseppe   42
Schaefer, Ina   1, 16
Severyn, Aliaksei   34
Spalazzese, Romina   79
Steffen, Bernhard   1, 61
Sykes, Daniel   79

Yskout, Koen   25